IS IT REASONABLE TO BELIEVE THERE IS A GOD?

A God That Has Sent
A Message
To Us

G. Michael Cocoris

© 2025 by G. Michael Cocoris

All rights reserved. This publication may not be reproduced (in whole or in part, edited, or revised) in any way, form, or means, including, but not limited to electronic, mechanical, photocopying, recording or any kind of storage and retrieval system for sale, except for brief quotations in printed reviews, without the written permission of G. Michael Cocoris, 2016 Euclid #20, Santa Monica, CA 90405, michaelcocoris@gmail.com, or his appointed representatives. Permission is hereby granted, however, for the reproduction of the whole or parts of the whole without changing the content in any way for free distribution, provided all copies contain this copyright notice in its entirety. Permission is also granted to charge for the cost of copying.

Unless otherwise indicated, all Scripture quotations are taken from the New King James Version ®, Copyright © 1979, 1980, 1982 by Thomas Nelson, Inc. Used by permission. All rights reserved.

Exterior and interior design by John T. Cocoris.

TABLE OF CONTENTS

Preface

Chapter	1	Introduction	1
Chapter	2	It Is Reasonable To Believe God Exists	5
Chapter	3	It Is Reasonable To Believe God Has Sent A Message	13
Chapter	4	It Is Reasonable To Believe God's Message Is Accurate Part 1	39
Chapter	5	It Is Reasonable To Believe God's Message Is Accurate Part 2	103
Chapter	6	God's Message To You	115
Chapter	7	Conclusion	129

Appendix: Early References To The
    New Testament   133
Bibliopraphy   135
About The Author   143

PREFACE

Having spoken to people about the Lord for over 65 years, I have encountered a wide range of objections. How do you know there is a God? How do you know the Bible is the Word of God? How do you know we have the correct number of books in the Bible? Are there books in the Bible that should not be there? The book of Esther does not mention the word "God." Based on that, a missionary I met said the book of Esther should not be in the Bible. Are there books that should be in the Bible but aren't? Some translations of the Bible include notes stating that this verse is not found in the best manuscripts. That means that not all manuscripts agree. How do we know which manuscripts are accurate? Over the years, I have investigated each of these questions to determine the truth.

For decades, I have argued that it is reasonable to believe in the existence of God based on the cosmological, teleological, and anthropological arguments for His existence. I first learned those arguments for the existence of God while in college, taking courses in philosophy, and have used them in multiple conversations. On two occasions, at the beginning of a conversation with someone who did not believe in God, I was able to start with those arguments and ultimately lead the person to Christ.

Many years ago, I heard a minister speak about his book on the canon of the Bible. "Canon" is a theological word used for determining which books should be in the Bible. He had written his doctoral dissertation on the subject. As I listened to him, I found myself not buying what he was selling. Since I had encountered this subject before but had not personally studied it, I decided to investigate it for myself. I read articles and books, and as I have often done, wrote a paper entitled "The Formation of the Bible." More recently, it has been published. It is available on Amazon, Barnes & Noble, and my website, insightsfromtheword.com, at a discount.

My interest in the biblical text began during my college years. As I will explain later in this book, there are two basic theories. One category of manuscripts has been referred to as the Textus Receptus, the Syrian text, the Traditional Text, the Majority Text, and the Byzantine Text. The King James Version and the New King James Version are based on that text type. The other category of manuscripts is called the Critical Text and the Alexandrian Text. All popular modern English translations are based on that text type, including the Revised Standard Version, the New American Standard Bible, the New International Version, the English Standard Version, etc.

In college, I accepted the Alexandrian text type as being the best text type. In seminary, I was taught that the Alexandrian text type was superior. After I graduated from seminary, I practiced what is known as "textual criticism," believing that the Alexandrian text type is the more accurate representation of the New Testament. Then, a few years after I graduated, I bought a book, thinking it was a commentary. It wasn't. It was a book on the New Testament text issue. What I read prompted me to study, which led to a change in my perspective. I concluded that the evidence favored the Byzantine text type. The name of that book is *The Last Twelve Verses of the Gospel According to S. Mark* by John William Burgon.

Preface

Since then, I periodically read articles and books on the subject of the New Testament text. As I did that, I took notes, wrote an article I never released, and stuffed it all in a folder. A few years ago, the subject came up in a question-and-answer session. As a result of that experience, I reviewed all the material I had collected over the years, including the article I had written. I rewrote the article and published a book titled *The Greek New Testament Issue*. It is available on Amazon, Barnes & Noble, and my website, insightsfromtheword.com, at a discount.

At this point in my life, I have written a commentary and preached through every book of the Bible. All of that and more is free on my website, insightsfromtheword.com. I have studied and written extensively on the existence of God and the books and texts of the Bible for decades, but I have never put those last three subjects together in one place. Hence, this book.

I am persuaded that it is reasonable to believe that there is a God, that God has sent us a message, and that we have an accurate copy of that message. As I will explain in the introduction, I am not claiming that we have so-called "scientific" proof. I am claiming it is reasonable to believe. Here is how I arrived at the conclusion. You have to decide for yourself whether or not you think it is reasonable to believe.

G. Michael Cocoris
Santa Monica, CA

Chapter 1

Introduction

The ultimate question in life is, "Is there a God?" It is generally assumed that to know whether or not something is true, there must be proof. That raises the question of what constitutes proof? To complicate matters, there are various types of evidence. What are they?

Mathematical Proof

Mathematical proof uses logical arguments to demonstrate that the statement is always true. It uses axioms and theorems. An axiom is a proposition that is an established, accepted, or self-evidently true. A theorem is a declaration that can be determined to be true using mathematical operations. Pythagoras developed the Pythagorean theorem, which states that in a right-angled triangle, the square of the length of the hypotenuse (the side opposite the right angle) is equal to the sum of the squares of the lengths of the other two sides. Most would argue that mathematics is not an appropriate tool for establishing or refuting the existence of God.

Scientific Proof

"Scientific proof" is not a concept in science. Mathematics speaks of proofs. Science is based on repeatable experiments. A scientific

Introduction

claim is supported (or not supported) by repeatable empirical evidence—observations, experiments, and measurements. When sufficiently high-quality, repeatable evidence consistently supports a hypothesis, it is accepted as scientific knowledge. However, well-established theories remain tentative, meaning they could be revised or replaced if better evidence emerges. So, when people say "scientific proof," they mean: repeatable evidence that supports a thesis.

To illustrate, suppose I had two glasses filled with liquids and said that if I poured them together into a third glass, there would be an explosion, and you said, "Prove it." To prove that what I said was accurate, I would pour the contents of the two glasses into a third glass. That is scientific proof because it can be repeated over and over again.

So-called "scientific proof" cannot be used to prove or disprove the existence of God because God is not repeatable.

Logical Proof

Logical proof is based on reasoning to show that a claim must be valid. It uses deductive logic. If the premise is true, the logical conclusion must be true. Aristotle writes of three forms of proof: logos, pathos, and ethos (Book I, Chapter 2). Logos is the logic of the argument. Ethos is the credibility of the speaker. Pathos refers to the emotional appeal made to the audience. These are methods of persuasion, but his logos is a type of proof. This approach has been used in discussions of God's existence.

Legal Proof

Legal proof is sufficient evidence to persuade a judge or jury of the truth of a claim. The evidence can be physical, documentary, testimonial, or circumstantial. Legal proof isn't about absolute certainty, but about meeting a legal standard of proof (SOP), which depends on the type of case.

- In civil cases, the usually required proof is a **"preponderance of evidence**," meaning it is more likely that the claim is valid than not true.
- In some civil or special cases, the standard is **"clear and convincing evidence**," which is substantially and significantly more likely to be true than not true.
- In criminal cases, the prosecution must prove guilt **"beyond a reasonable doubt**," not beyond "any doubt," a "possible doubt," or an "imaginary doubt," but a doubt based on reason and common sense, arising from the evidence or lack of it.

Here's how it works. The judge instructs the jury to consider all the direct evidence (eyewitness testimony) and circumstantial evidence and draw the most reasonable inference from the evidence presented. They are not to consider what they think might be another possibility. They are to make a decision based on the evidence presented. "Our judicial system trusted folks like you and me to examine the testimony of experts and come to a reasonable conclusion about the truth.... Jurors need to be able to listen to the experts, carefully evaluate the evidence, and draw the most reasonable inference" (Wallace, p. 259).

People on a jury do not have to be experts. There are professional cooks, but people do not have to be professional chefs to prepare a meal. They just need to follow a recipe. Likewise, people do not have to be experts in history, literature, archaeology, or theology to determine if God exists. They just need to be like a jury that hears a case and draws a reasonable inference from the evidence presented.

Practical Proof

Practical proof is that which convinces people in ordinary daily life that something is true. A receipt proves a purchase. An ID proves identity. This type of proof typically involves physical evidence.

Summary: Mathematical and scientific types of "proof" do not apply in the quest for determining God's existence, but logical and legal "proofs" have been used.

In other words, is it reasonable to believe there is a God? When reading this material, assume that you are on a jury. Consider the case being presented, and determine what you think is a reasonable inference based solely on the evidence presented. The issue is not possibilities. The issue is: **based on the case presented, is it reasonable to believe** there is a God who has sent a message to us?

Chapter 2

It Is Reasonable To Believe God Exists

Is it reasonable to believe that God exists? One way to answer that question is to start with what we know exists and ask how it came into existence. We know the universe exists. How did it get here? What existed at the beginning? What are the possibilities?

One possibility is that at the beginning, there was nothing. That is not a reasonable answer, because nothing cannot produce something.

Another possibility is that the material universe always existed. It is eternal. An eternal material universe is not a reasonable explanation for *everything* because life exists in the universe and something material cannot produce life.

For example, a piece of marble cannot create a statue of a human being, much less a living human being.

That leaves a third possibility that, at the beginning, there was some kind of life. That means that either life is eternal or life and the material universe are eternal. In either case, life is eternal.

Now the question becomes, is it more reasonable to believe that life and the material universe are eternal or that some kind of life produced the material universe? The nature of what exists, the material universe (the subject of this chapter), indicates that it is reasonable to believe that some form of life produced it. The name given to that type of life is God. This explanation says that what we know exists (the material universe and the life forms that are in it) had a cause (God). Three effects indicate a cause. Those three effects indicate it is reasonable to believe that life (God) caused the material universe.

Cosmological Argument

The physical universe is an effect that must have had a cause. If there is a painting, there must be a painter. If there is a building, there must be a builder. There is a universe. Thus, there must be a universe maker. The philosophy department at a university refers to this as the cosmological argument for the existence of God. The cosmos, the universe, is an effect caused by God.

Aristotle used this argument. He said that a given motion must be caused by another motion, which was caused by another motion, ad infinitum, but infinite regression is impossible. Therefore, there must be a first cause. There must be a motion not caused by something that did not move—an unmoved mover or an unmoved first mover. (The foundational principles for the Unmoved Mover are explored in Aristotle's work entitled Physics, particularly in Book VIII. The most comprehensive treatment of the Unmoved Mover is found in his Metaphysics, Book XII, Chapters 6-7.) Wallace puts it like this, "This 'uncaused first cause' must exist outside of space, time, and matter (as nothing has ever been observed to cause itself to exist" (Wallace, p. 60).

In short, the universe is an effect that requires a cause. When talking to students, I have used my watch as an illustration. I take off my watch, put it in their hand, and ask them what they know,

It is Reasonable To Believe God Exists

because the watch is in their possession. They make observations, telling me the time, the color of the watch, the kind of watchband, etc. When they are done, I ask, "What else do you know?" I then pointed out that I know something they did not mention, namely, because that watch exists, there must be a watchmaker. Likewise, since the universe exists, it is reasonable to believe that there is a Creator.

Teleological Argument

Design in the physical universe is an effect that must have had a cause. The world not only exists, it also has design. Philosophically, this is called the teleological argument for the existence of God.

There is order and design in the universe. The earth turns over at more than 1,000 miles per hour. The moon, meanwhile, is circling the earth at 365 miles per hour, making one complete circle every 27⅓ days. Additionally, the earth, with the moon revolving around it, is revolving around the sun at 68,400 miles per hour (approximately 19 miles per second). It makes one complete revolution every 24 hours and covers approximately 6,000,000 miles annually.

Meanwhile, the sun is rotating around another sun (a star called Halcyone) at the speed of 422,000 miles per day. The circumference of these circles is so great that it takes thousands of years to complete one cycle. Why doesn't something get off track and crash into something? What a "fender-bender" that would be! After scanning the heavens, Sir James Jeans, the great astronomer, declared, "The universe seems to have been designed by a pure mathematician."

There is order and design within the atom. "The precise

relationship between protons, neutrons, and electrons appeared to be fine-tuned and calibrated" (Wallace, p. 61). "DNA contains characteristics that ... are best explained by the creative activity of an intelligent designer" (Wallace, p. 63).

Order and design do not just happen. Things go from order to disorder. Order and design indicate some mind or intelligence at work. Order means an organizer. Design indicates a designer. The order and design in the material universe indicate that the material universe is not eternal. It had to have had an intelligent cause.

To illustrate, I use a watch. I point out that it takes intelligence to make the watch—more intelligence than I have. Likewise, the order and design of the universe indicate an intelligent designer.

Anthropological Argument

Human beings are an effect that must have had a cause. The presence of people on this planet requires a cause—a personal cause. This complex creature, called humans, can trust, love, and hope. That effect necessitates a personal cause. Something impersonal has never been known to produce anything personal. In other words, in the case of humans, the cause was someone, not something.

At the beginning, there was something, not nothing, because nothing cannot produce something. Design in the material universe indicates that the material universe is not eternal. Therefore, since there had to have been something at the beginning, that something was life, and that life is eternal. The idea that the material universe has always existed is akin to saying that two rocks produced a rabbit. I don't have enough faith to believe that. It is easier to believe that a living, intelligent designer created the world and the

It is Reasonable To Believe God Exists

life forms that inhabit it.

Summary: The material universe, order, design, and humans are effects that indicate a powerful, intelligent, personal cause. Therefore, it is reasonable to believe that a personal God caused what exists in the universe.

Atheists say there is no God, but atheism is illogical. One of the laws of logic is that one cannot prove a universal negative, and atheism is a universal negative. All an atheist has is questions, theories, and a great deal of faith, which is not supported by evidence.

Bertrand Russell, the famous atheist, admitted he could not prove his position. He said, "As a philosopher, if I were speaking to a purely philosophic audience, I would say I ought to describe myself as an agnostic because I do not think there is a conclusive argument by which one can prove that there is not a God" (Russell, American Atheist, August 1978).

Agnostics say nothing is known or can be known of the existence or nature of God or anything beyond material phenomena, but isn't it illogical to limit oneself to "natural phenomena?" Remember, two rocks can't produce a rabbit, nor can material phenomena produce life, love, trust, and hope.

The English biologist Thomas Henry Huxley said that he originally coined the word agnostic in 1869 "to denote people who, like [himself], confess themselves to be hopelessly ignorant concerning a variety of matters [including the matter of God's existence], about which metaphysicians and theologians, both orthodox and heterodox, dogmatize with the utmost confidence." Note: agnostics are "hopelessly ignorant" because they limit the possibilities to the material universe.

Is It Reasonable To Believe There Is A God?

On the other hand, it is reasonable to believe in a personal God. Admittedly, there is no conclusive "scientific proof" that a God exists. At the same time, it is reasonable to believe in the existence of a God. There are reasons, good reasons. There is logic, excellent logic.

Consider the explanation of a former atheist. Frank Pastore thought anyone who believed in God was uneducated, naïve, or stupid. When Christians challenged him, he set out to disprove theism, which he didn't think would take long. In the process of trying to do that, he encountered four factors he had never considered. He calls them "four big bangs."

The first "big bang" is the universe, the cosmos. That's something from nothing! Furthermore, he realized that the "theoretical cosmological big bang" only produced matter and energy. It does not explain the origin of life. That requires, in his words, "another something-from-nothing leap of faith."

The second big bang is life, a biological big bang. Granted, science has made "mind-boggling advancements" in physics, biology, and chemistry. He says, "We've learned a lot about how to manipulate life forms, how to add and subtract DNA material, even map the human genome, but we have no idea how to literally create life from dead stuff."

The third big bang is the existence of humanity, an anthropological big bang. He points out that there is a vast difference between bacteria, plants, animals, and human beings. We do not have a way to account for the differences between man and animals.

The fourth big bang is the nature of human beings, a psychological big bang. Lower life forms may have a brain and a central nervous system, but how does that become "the mind of a Michelangelo, a Shakespeare, a Beethoven? Come on, animals don't do art, and they don't appreciate beauty. But the problem is even more basic than that. How do you account for free will and introspection, let alone man's pressing existential drive to ask, 'why?' Well, we're going to need some kind of psychological fourth big bang to account for man's moral and aesthetic sense—his search for meaning, significance, and purpose, and of course his appreciation for the true, the good, and the beautiful."

Pastore concludes, "So, I, like you, have a choice. It's either faith in these four big bangs ... or faith in some kind of creator God behind it all. So, next time someone asks you, 'Hey, what about the big bang?' make sure you ask them: 'Which one? The cosmological, biological, anthropological, or psychological?'" (This is an edited version of his video at https://www.prageru.com/video/does-god-exist-4-new-arguments. He tells his whole story in his book *Shattered*.)

This is not a new idea. For thousands of years, people have argued that it is reasonable to believe in the existence of a God due to the existence of the universe. Two thousand years ago, Paul claimed that "the living God ... made the heaven, the earth, the sea, and all things that are in them.... He did not leave Himself without witness, in that He did good, gave us rain from heaven and fruitful seasons, filling our hearts with food and gladness" (Acts 14:15-17). He also pointed out that invisible aspects of God can be clearly seen in the things that are made. He said, "For since the creation of the world, His invisible attributes are clearly seen being understood by the things that are made, even His eternal power and Godhead so that they are without excuse" (Romans 1:20). Creation reveals a Creator. Look at the world and see the sun, stars, sea, moon, mountain, and man. That indicates a sun-maker, a star-maker, a sea-maker, a moon-maker, a mountain-maker, and a man-maker, who is powerful and intelligent.

Twenty-seven hundred years ago, Isaiah wrote, "Lift up your eyes on high, and see who has created these things, who brings out their host by number; He calls them all by name, by the greatness of His might and the strength of His power" (Isaiah 40:26).

Three thousand years ago, David declared, "The heavens declare the glory of God (Psalm 19:1). It is reasonable to suggest that people should look up to see the power, intelligence, and glory of the Creator.

In the final analysis, one must exercise faith. God designed it that way. Hebrews 11:6 says, "Without faith, it is impossible to please Him, for he who comes to God must believe that He is and that He is a rewarder of those who diligently seek Him." It is one thing to know that there is a God; it is another thing to know the God who is. Is that possible? Keep reading,

Chapter 3

It Is Reasonable To Believe God Has Sent A Message

If there is an intelligent designer called God who created the universe, including people, has He sent us a message? Are there reasons to believe that God has sent human beings a message? Where would you go to find such a message? The study of God is not in English, math, or PE classes. It is the field of religion.

Hinduism does not have a founder. The Vedas, the sacred text of Hinduism, were composed from about 1500 B.C. to 500 B.C. Hinduism is more of a philosophy than a set of beliefs. Within it are atheism, monotheism, polytheism, and pantheism. The notions of reincarnation and karma come from it, but there is no claim that a Creator has sent people a message.

Buddha (563 to 483 BC) founded Buddhism, but it is also more of a philosophy than a religion. The *Encyclopedia Britannica* (online edition) says it is a "nontheistic religion." Buddha saw suffering and wanted to eliminate it. So, he came up with the Four Noble Truths and the Noble Eightfold Path. The truth of suffering is that everything is suffering (birth is suffering, aging is suffering, illness is suffering, death is suffering; union with what is displeasing is suffering; separation from what is pleasing is suffering; not getting what one wants is suffering). The truth of the origin of suffering is craving for sensual pleasures, craving for becoming, and craving for dis-becoming. The truth of the cessation of suffering is the cessation of that same craving, the giving up and relinquishing it, freedom from it, and non-reliance on it. The truth of the way leading to the cessation of suffering is this Noble Eightfold Path: right view, right intention, right speech, right action, right livelihood, right effort, right mindfulness, and right concentration. Buddhism does not claim that a Creator has sent a message to us.

Confucius (551–479 BC) was a Chinese politician and philosopher. His philosophy was personal morality, social relationships, justice, and sincerity. He taught family loyalty, respect for elders, and ancestor worship—no message from God here.

Zarathustra, known to the Greeks as Zoroaster, founded Zoroastrianism in Persia in the 6th century BC. Zoroaster reformed Persian polytheism with his teachings about the highest god, Ahura Mazdā, and his primeval clash with Angra Mainyu, the Destructive Spirit. Scholars differ on whether Zoroastrianism is monotheistic, polytheistic, henotheistic (the belief in one primary deity while acknowledging the existence of other deities), or a combination of all three.

John Wilson (1804-1875), a Christian missionary in British India, claimed "Zoroaster never had a genuine divine commission (or ever claimed such a role), never performed miracles, or uttered prophecies, and the story of his life is 'comparatively modern fables and fiction'" (https://en.wikipedia.org/wiki/Criticism_of_Zoroastrianism#:~:text=In%20the%20early%2019th%20century,comparatively%20modern%20fables%20and%20 fiction%22).

Only three world religions claim that God has sent a message to us: Judaism, Christianity, and Islam.

Judaism is based on the Hebrew Scriptures written from 1447 to about 400 BC. The Hebrew Scriptures are identical to the Protestant Old Testament. Christianity accepts the Scripture of Judaism as valid.

Muhammad (ca. 570-632) founded Islam. He had 11 wives and two concubines. Some scholars argue that concubines were considered wives. He married Khadija, his wealthy employer, in 595, when he was 25 and she was either 28 or 41. They had six children. She died in 619. He then married Sawdah (619–632), when she was between the ages of 40 and 55, Aisha (620–632), when she was six years old, Hafsah (625–632), Zaynab bint Khuzayma (625–626), Hind (625–632), Zaynab bint Jahsh (627–632), Juwayriya (628–632), Ramla (628–632), Safiyya (629–632), and Maymunah (629–632). Rayhana (627–631) and Maria (628–632) were either additional wives or concubines.

Mohammed personally participated in war. The exact number is debated. Some sources say nine, including the Battle of Badr (624), the Battle of Uhud (625), the Battle of the Trench (627), and the Conquest of Mecca (630). Other sources indicate that he participated in 20 to 30 wars, with the generally cited number being 27 or 29. The exact number of battles he ordered is also debated. The number ranges from 40 to 70 or even more. The variations in these numbers stem from how events are defined and counted. Some accounts combine events that happened around the same time or place.

Mohammed personally killed people. The most widely agreed-upon case is the Ubayy ibn Khalaf report, which states that in the Battle of Uhud (625), Mohammed struck Ubayy, one of his fiercest enemies in Mecca, with a spear during the battle, and Ubayy died on the way back to Mecca. Again, the numbers are disputed. Some Islamic sources put the number he executed at 40, while others report 600 to 700.

Mohammed claims he received his first revelation from the archangel Gabriel in AD 610 while in a cave near Mecca. Gabriel informed him that he was God's prophet and gave him the Quran, the sacred text of Islam. Muslims believe in one God, Allah, and that Muhammad was the final prophet. The Five Pillars of Islam are the declaration of faith, praying five times daily, giving in charity, fasting, and performing a pilgrimage to Mecca.

The evidence for the Quran is said to be: 1) The Quran is like no other book; only God could have written it. 2) The Quran is perfectly preserved; there are no changes in it (Quran 15:9 states, "Indeed, We have sent down the Reminder, and indeed We are its guardian," meaning Allah promised the Quran will remain preserved throughout time. 15:9). 3) The Quran contains scientific knowledge beyond Mohammed's knowledge.

None of that is true. Ibn al-Rawandi (d. 911) dismissed the Quran as "not the speech of someone with wisdom; [it] contain[s] contradictions, errors, and absurdities" (Michael Cook, *The Koran: A Very Short Introduction*. Oxford University Press, 2000). Furthermore, Quran 5:72 says, "Verily, whosoever sets up partners in worship with Allah, then Allah has forbidden Paradise for him, and the Fire will be his abode." In other words, Muslims who believe that Jesus is God go to hell.

The other possibility is Christianity, that is, Jesus Christ. On July 11, 1926, at a youth meeting at the Shrine Auditorium in Los Angeles, James Allan Frances, the Pastor of the First Baptist

Church of Los Angeles, said something in a sermon that has become well known as "One Solitary Life." It reads as follows:

> Here is a young man who was born in an obscure village, the child of a peasant woman. He grew up in another village. He worked in a carpenter shop until He was thirty, and then for three years, He was an itinerant preacher. He never wrote a book. He never held an office. He never owned a home. He never had a family. He never went to college. He never put His foot inside a big city. He never traveled 200 miles from the place where He was born. He never did one of the things that usually accompany greatness. He had no credentials but Himself.
>
> While He was still a young man, the tide of public opinion turned against Him. His friends ran away. He was turned over to His enemies. He went through the mockery of a trial. He was nailed to the cross between two thieves. While He was dying, His executioners gambled for the only piece of property He had on earth, and that was His coat. When He was dead, He was laid in a borrowed grave through the pity of a friend.
>
> Nineteen centuries have come and gone, and today He is the central figure of the human race and the leader of the column of progress. I am far within the mark when I say that all the armies that ever marched, and all the navies that ever sailed, and all the parliaments that ever sat, and all the kings that ever reigned, put together, have not affected the life of man upon this earth as has that One Solitary Life.

The sacred book of Christianity is the Bible. It claims to be a divinely inspired message from God, the creator of the universe.

The first thing the Bible says is, "In the beginning God created the heavens and the earth" (Genesis 1:1). The psalmist declares, "May you be blessed by the LORD, who made heaven and earth" (Psalm 115:15). The Creator has communicated to us via the Bible.

Over 3,000 times, the authors of the Old Testament declare: "Thus says the Lord" or "The LORD says." David, the author of half of the Psalms, said, "The Spirit of the LORD spoke by me" (2 Samuel 23:2). The New Testament uses the phrase "the word of God" to refer to the teachings of Jesus, the preaching of the apostles, and the writings of Paul and Peter.

Paul said, "The things which I write to you are the commandments of the Lord" (1 Corinthians 14:37). Referring to hearing God speak out loud on the mount of Transfiguration (Matthew 17:1-5), Peter wrote, "For we did not follow cunningly devised fables when we made known to you the power and coming of our Lord Jesus Christ, but were eyewitnesses of His majesty. For He received from God the Father honor and glory when such a voice came to Him from the Excellent Glory: 'This is My beloved Son, in whom I am well pleased.' And we heard this voice which came from heaven when we were with Him on the holy mountain. And so we have the prophetic word confirmed, which you do well to heed as a light that shines in a dark place, until the day dawns and the morning star rises in your hearts" (2 Peter 1:16-19).

"All Scripture is given by inspiration of God, and is profitable for doctrine, for reproof, for correction, for instruction in righteousness" (2 Timothy 3:16). "Prophecy never came by the will of man, but holy men of God spoke as they were moved by the Holy Spirit" (2 Peter 1:21).

Is it reasonable to believe that the Bible is a message from God? Is the Bible like any other book written by human beings, or is it reasonable to believe that God was involved in the writing of the Bible?

Prophecy

It is reasonable to believe that God was involved in the writing of the Bible because the Old Testament contains predictions of the coming of a Messiah hundreds of years before He arrived. Those predictions were fulfilled in the coming of Jesus. The certainty of the Bible is based on fulfilled prophecy.

In 1447 BC, the Old Testament prophesied that the Messiah would be **a man, not an angel**. Genesis 3:15 says, "And I will put enmity between you and the woman and between your seed and her seed; he shall bruise your head, and you shall bruise his heel." The ancient rabbis said that the seed of the woman is the Messiah.

In 1447 BC, the Old Testament prophesied that the Messiah would be **a Jew, not a Gentile**. Genesis 22:18 says, "In your seed, all the nations of the earth shall be blessed because you have obeyed My voice." The ancient rabbis said that the seed of Abraham is the Messiah.

In 1447 BC, the Old Testament prophesied that the Messiah would be **from the tribe of Judah**. Genesis 49:10 says, "The scepter shall not depart from Judah, nor a lawgiver from between his feet, until Shiloh comes; and to Him shall be the obedience of the people." Ancient rabbis said Shiloh was another name for the Messiah and that He would come from the tribe of Judah.

In 1000 BC, the Old Testament prophesied that the Messiah was **the Son of God**. Psalm. 2:6-8 says, "Yet I have set My King on My holy hill of Zion. I will declare the decree: The LORD has said to Me, 'You are My Son, Today I have begotten You. Ask of Me, and I will give You the nations for Your inheritance, and the ends of the earth for Your possession.'" Ancient Rabbis said this passage is Messianic.

In 1000 BC, the Old Testament prophesied that the Messiah **would be resurrected**. Psalm 16:10 says, "For You will not leave my soul in Sheol, nor will You allow Your Holy One to see corruption." Ancient Rabbis said this passage is Messianic.

In 925 BC, the Old Testament prophesied that the Messiah **would be a descendant of David**. Second Samuel 7:12 says, "When your days are fulfilled, and you rest with your fathers, I will set up your seed after you, who will come from your body, and I will establish His kingdom." Ancient rabbis said the Messiah would be the Son of David.

About 725 BC, the Old Testament prophesied that the Messiah would be **born in Bethlehem**. Micah 5:2 says, "But you, Bethlehem Ephrathah, though you are little among the thousands of Judah, Yet out of you shall come forth to Me the One to be Ruler in Israel, Whose goings forth are from of old, from everlasting." According to ancient rabbis, the Messiah was expected to be born in Bethlehem.

Around 680 BC, the Old Testament foresaw that He would be **born of a virgin**. Isaiah 7:14 says, "Therefore the Lord Himself will give you a sign: Behold, the virgin shall conceive and bear a Son, and shall call His name Immanuel."

In 680 BC, the Old Testament prophesied that the Messiah was **the Son of God**. Isaiah 9:6 says, "For unto us a Child is born, unto us a Son is given; and the government will be upon His shoulder. And His name will be called Wonderful, Counselor, Mighty God, Everlasting Father, Prince of Peace." Ancient Rabbis said this passage is Messianic.

In 680 BC, the Old Testament prophesied that the Messiah **would die for others**. Isaiah 53:6 says, "All we like sheep have gone astray; we have turned, everyone, to his own way; and the LORD has laid on Him the iniquity of us all." Ancient Rabbis said this passage is Messianic.

About 530 BC, the Old Testament foretold **the time of His arrival**. Because of their sin, the nation of Israel was exiled to Babylon. Jeremiah said that it would last for 70 years. At the end of 70 years, when Daniel asked, "What would happen next?" He was told, "Seventy weeks are determined on your people and for your holy city …. Know therefore and understand, that from the going forth of the command to restore and build Jerusalem until Messiah the Prince, there shall be seven weeks and sixty-two weeks; the street shall be built again, and the wall, even in troublesome times. And after sixty-two weeks, Messiah shall be cut off, but not for Himself; and the people of the prince who is to come shall destroy the city and the sanctuary. The end of it shall be with a flood, and till the end of the war desolations are determined" (Daniel 9:24-27).

This passage states that seventy "weeks" are determined for the Jewish people and the city of Jerusalem. What is the meaning of "seventy weeks?" The Hebrew word translated "weeks" means "seven." It could be seven weeks, seven months, or seven years. The context demands that the seventy sevens are years. In other words, God's program for Israel involves another 490 years (7 x 70 = 490).

The 490 years will begin from "the going forth of the command to restore and build Jerusalem" (Danial 9:25). Furthermore, from the beginning, "until Messiah the Prince" will be sixty-nine weeks (483 years; see Danial 9:25). After that "Messiah shall be cut off, but not for Himself" (Danial 9:26). In other words, this Old Testament passage is giving a date for the coming of the Messiah after which time He will be "cut off, but not for Himself," a reference to His death. (The Hebrew word translated "cut off" was used of the death penalty; see Leviticus 7:20, etc.). The only question is, when do the 483 years begin? There are four possibilities for dating the beginning of this time frame.

 The Decree of Cyrus (Ezra 1) 539 BC
 The Decree of Darius (Ezra 6) 519 BC
 The Decree of Artaxerxes (Ezra 7) 458 BC
 The Decree of Artaxerxes (Nehemiah 2) 445 BC

Each of these has been suggested as the beginning of the 490 years. Without going into detail, the Decree of Artaxerxes (Ezra 7) in 458 BC is the one that fits all the perimeters. At first glance, it seems that the Decree of Artaxerxes concerned the Temple (Ezra 7:19-20), but it included much more than that. Artaxerxes said they could do "whatever seems good to you," "according to the will of God" (Ezra 7:18). Later, Ezra thanked God that He "did not forsake us in our bondage; but He extended mercy to us in the sight of the kings of Persia, to revive us, to repair the house of our God, to rebuild its ruins, and to give us a wall in Judah and Jerusalem" (Ezra 9:9).

Moreover, it perfectly fits the coming of Christ. Calling this the traditional view, Boutflower dates the decree in 457 BC and concludes that 483 years later, in AD 26, the Messiah was made manifest to Israel (Boutflower, pp. 186-191). Archer also dates the decree in 457 BC, but he says AD 25 is the time of Christ's ministry (Archer, p. 387). Wood states that the decree was issued in 458 BC, and the 483 years ended in AD 26, as only one year elapsed between 1 BC and AD (Wood, pp. 252-254).

These predictions that the Messiah would be a man, a Jew, from the tribe of Judah, from the family of David, from the city of Bethlehem, from a virgin, the Son of God, who would die and be resurrected at a specific time, were perfectly fulfilled in the coming of Jesus Christ. There is nothing like this in the history of the world. Other ancient and modern predictions give only one or two particulars expressed in general and ambiguous terms. Throughout all history, there is not a single instance of a prediction, expressed in unequivocal language, which has been fulfilled—except those found in the Scripture.

The odds of one human being fulfilling just eight of these prophecies are 1 x 1 x 10 to the 17th power. That's one in 100,000,000,000,000,000. To put this into perspective, imagine we have enough silver dollars to cover the entire state of Texas two feet deep. We put an "X" on one of those silver dollars, hide it, and stir the whole pile. Then we blindfold a man in Dallas and tell him he can go as far as he wants, but he must pick up the one silver dollar we marked. That's the same chance as a human being fulfilling these specific prophecies, many of which he would have no control over, such as his place of birth. If forty-eight of these prophecies were true of one man, the odds increase to 1x10 to the 157th power (McDowell, pp. 144, 167).

The Resurrection of Jesus Christ

It is reasonable to believe that God was involved in the writing of the Bible, given that Jesus rose from the dead. The bodily resurrection of Jesus Christ is unique. Abraham, the father of Judaism, died around 2000 BC. No claim of a resurrection for him has ever been made. His tomb has been carefully preserved for over 4,000 years. According to tradition, it is in Hebron. A Muslim Mosque sits on the site.

None of the sources for the life of Buddha has ever claimed a resurrection for him. The Mahaparinibbana Sutta says that when he died, it was "with that utter passing away in which nothing whatever remains behind." Muhammad died on June 8, 632, at the age of sixty-one in Medina, and his tomb is visited annually by thousands of devout Muslims. Still, no claim is made of a bodily resurrection.

Moreover, "there is no resurrection in nature. We may just as truly say that everything is as the grass which blooms and quickly fades. Every spring carries within it autumn, for every birth, there is death" (Thielecke, cited by S. Lewis Johnson).

The case for the resurrection of Jesus consists of three issues: 1) Jesus was executed; He actually died. 2) The tomb was empty; He rose from the dead. 3) Eyewitnesses saw the resurrected Jesus. Furthermore, it is worth noting that ancient secular sources also mention the resurrection of Jesus Christ. All of this is objective proof of the bodily resurrection of Jesus Christ.

Execution Jesus was executed; He actually died. Matthew wrote, "They crucified him" (Matthew 27:35), and "Jesus cried out again with a loud voice, and yielded up His spirit" (Matthew 27:50). Mark recorded, "They crucified Him" (Mark 15:24) and "Jesus cried out with a loud voice, and breathed His last (Mark 15:37). Luke penned, "They crucified Him" (Luke 23:33) and "When Jesus cried out with a loud voice, He said, 'Father into your hands I commit My spirit.' Having said this, He breathed His last" (Luke 23:46). John reported, "Then the soldiers, when they had crucified Jesus, took His garments, and made four parts, to each soldier part" (John 19:23) and "bowing His head, He gave up His spirit" (John 19:30). Note, Matthew, Mark, Luke, and John say that Jesus was crucified. There is no record anywhere of anyone surviving a Roman crucifixion. Jesus died.

The soldiers were convinced that Jesus died. "Then the soldiers came and broke the legs of the first and of the other who was crucified with Him. But when they came to Jesus and saw that He was already dead, they did not break His legs" (John 19:32-33). They did not break His legs because they concluded He was already dead.

Pontius Pilate was convinced that Jesus died. When Joseph of Arimathea asked Pilate for the body of Jesus (Mark 15:43), "Pilate marveled that He was already dead; and summoning the centurion, he asked him if He had been dead for some time. So when he found out from the centurion, he granted the body to Joseph (Mark 15:44-45).

Ancient sources outside the Bible mention Jesus' death. "Many first-century and early second-century *unfriendly* Roman sources (i.e., Thallus, Tacitus, Mara Bar-Serapion, and Phlegon and Jewish sources (i.e., Josephus and the Babylonian Talmud) affirm and acknowledge that Jesus was crucified and died" (Wallace, p. 43, italics his). To be specific, Josephus (AD 37-ca. 100), a Jewish historian, mentions Jesus' death, specifically His condemnation by Pontius Pilate (see Antiquities of the Jews, 18, 3, 3 at; https://www.gutenberg.org/files/2848/2848-h/2848-h.htm). Other non-biblical, non-Christian references to the death of Jesus include Tacitus (Annals 15:44), Suetonius (Claudius 25), and Pliny the Younger (Letter to Trajan).

After investigating the death of Jesus, the American Medical Association's secular, scientific, peer-reviewed medical journal concluded, "Modern medical interpretation of the historical evidence indicates that Jesus was dead when taken down from the cross" (JAMA, March 21, 1986; https://jamanetwork.com/journals/jama/article-abstract/403315#google_vignette).

A university professor said, "Any denial of Jesus' historicity is maundering sensationalism by the uninformed and/or the dishonest" (Paul L. Maier; see his other comments below).

Empty Tomb The empty tomb indicates Jesus rose from the dead. First, note that after Jesus' burial, the tomb was guarded. Matthew says, "On the next day, which followed the Day of Preparation, the chief priests and Pharisees gathered together to Pilate, saying, 'Sir, we remember, while He was still alive, how that deceiver said, 'After three days I will rise.' Therefore, command that the tomb be made secure until the third day, lest His disciples come by night and steal Him away, and say to the people, 'He has risen from the dead.' So the last deception will be worse than the first.' Pilate said to them, 'You have a guard; go your way, make it as secure as you know how.' So they went and made the tomb secure, sealing the stone and setting the guard" (Matthew 27:62-66).

Two women were the first to see the empty tomb. Matthew says, "Now after the Sabbath, as the first day of the week began to dawn, Mary Magdalene and the other Mary came to see the tomb. And behold, there was a great earthquake; for an angel of the Lord descended from heaven, and came and rolled back the stone from the door, and sat on it. His countenance was like lightning, and his clothing as white as snow. And the guards shook for fear of him, and became like dead men. But the angel answered and said to the women, 'Do not be afraid, for I know that you seek Jesus who was crucified. He is not here; for He is risen, as He said. 'Come, see the place where the Lord lay, and go quickly and tell His disciples that He is risen from the dead, and indeed He is going before you into Galilee; there you will see Him. Behold, I have told you'" (Matthew 28:1-6). "But he [a young man] said to them [Mary Magdalene, Mary the mother of James, and Salome], "Do not be alarmed. You seek Jesus of Nazareth, who was crucified. He is risen! He is not here. See the place where they laid Him'" (Mark 16:6). Luke says, "Then they [the women] went in and did not find the body of the Lord Jesus" (Luke 24:43).

When Mary Magdalene told Peter and another disciple that the tomb was empty, "They both ran together, and the other disciple outran Peter and came to the tomb first. And he, stooping down and looking in, saw the linen cloths lying there; yet he did not go in. Then Simon Peter came, following him, and went into the tomb; and he saw the linen cloths lying there, and the handkerchief that had been around His head, not lying with the linen cloths, but folded together in a place by itself. Then the other disciple, who came to the tomb first, went in also; and he saw and believed"

(John 20:4-8).

Even the enemies of Jesus admitted that the tomb was empty. "Now, while they were going, behold, some of the guard came into the city and reported to the chief priests all the things that had happened. When they had assembled with the elders and consulted together, they gave a large sum of money to the soldiers, saying, 'Tell them, 'His disciples came at night and stole Him away while we slept.' And if this comes to the governor's ears, we will appease him and make you secure.' So they took the money and did as they were instructed; and this saying is commonly reported among the Jews until this day" (Matthew 28:11-15). To have to say the body was stolen proves the tomb was empty! The tomb was empty because Jesus rose from the dead. Keep reading.

Eyewitnesses Jesus was seen by eyewitnesses. Two women were the first to see the risen Jesus. "And as they (two women; see Matthew 28:1) went to tell His disciples, behold, Jesus met them, saying, 'Rejoice!' So, they came and held Him by the feet and worshiped Him" (Matthew 28:9; see also Mark 16:1, 9). Actually, on the first day after the resurrection, Jesus appeared to a number of people, including:

1. Mary Magdalene (Mark 16:9-11; John 20:11-18),
2. Another woman (Matthew 28:9-10),
3. Peter (Luke 24:34; 1 Corinthians 15:5),
4. Two men going to Emmaus (Mark 16:12; Luke 24:13-32)
5. Ten disciples in the upper room (Mark 16:14; John 20:19-25)

That was only the beginning. Paul says, "He was seen by Cephas, then by the twelve. After that, He was seen by over five hundred brethren at once, of whom the greater part remain to the present, but some have fallen asleep. After that, He was seen by James, then by all the apostles. Then last of all, He was seen by me also, as by one born out of due time" (1 Corinthians 15:5-8).

To say the same thing another way and add some additional details, on the First Day, the Lord appeared five times: to Mary, to another woman, to Peter, to the two on the way to Emmaus, and to the disciples, except Thomas (Matthew 28:9-15; Mark 16:9-14; Luke 24:13-43; John 20:11-25). The next Sunday, one week later, Jesus appeared to the disciples. This time, Thomas was present (John 20:26-31). He also appeared on other occasions (Matthew 28:16-20; Mark. 16:15-18; Luke 44-49; Jn. 21:1-25; Acts 1:3-8, 1 Corinthians. 15:6-7). Later, He appeared to the seven disciples beside the lake, to the 500 on a mount in Galilee, to James, and to the eleven disciples.

The apostles identified themselves as witnesses. In his sermon on the day of Pentecost, the apostle Peter testified, "This Jesus God raised up, of which we are all witnesses" (Acts 2:32). Later, in another sermon, he said the same thing. Speaking of Jesus, he said, "whom God raised from the dead, of which we are witnesses" (Acts 3:15). Still later, Peter and John said, "We cannot but speak the things we have seen and heard" (Acts 4:20). In another sermon, Peter said "We are witnesses of all things which He did both in the lands of the Jews and in Jerusalem" (Acts 10:39). Luke says "with great power the apostles gave witness to the resurrection of the Lord Jesus" (Acts 4:33).

The apostles viewed their writings as testimony of what they saw. For example, the apostle John wrote, "This is the disciple who testifies of these things and wrote these things, and we know that his testimony is true" (John 21:24). He also testified that he heard, saw with his eyes, looked upon, and his hands handled

Jesus (1 John 1:1). Peter wrote of himself that he was "a witness of the sufferings of Christ" (1 Peter 5:1) and one of the "eyewitnesses of his Majesty" (2 Peter 1:16), a reference to the Transfiguration of Christ.

One of the requirements for being an apostle was to have been a witness of Jesus. After the ascension, when the disciples were in the process of replacing Judas, Peter said they should choose one "who had accompanied us all the time that the Lord Jesus went in and out among us, beginning from the baptism of John to that day when He was taken up from us, one of these must become a witness with us of His resurrection" (Acts 2:21-22). Paul said, "Am I not an apostle? Am I not free? Have I not seen Jesus Christ our Lord? (1 Corinthians 9:1).

Some skeptics argue that the appearances of Jesus Christ after the resurrection were nothing more than hallucinations. If over 500 people saw the resurrected Christ "at once," the hallucination theory is wrong. Peter Kreeft points out, "Hallucinations usually happen only once, except to the insane. This one returned many times to ordinary people. Five hundred separate Elvis sightings may be dismissed, but if five hundred simple fishermen in Maine saw, touched, and talked with him at once, in the same town, that would be a different matter" (see this quotation and other arguments against this theory at https://www.josh.org/resurrection-theories-debunked/). The simple reality is that individuals have hallucinations. There are no examples of large groups of people having the same hallucination.

The conclusion is that there were eyewitnesses to the resurrection of Jesus Christ, who were not hallucinating. Moreover, it is reasonable to believe that these New Testament eyewitnesses of the resurrection of Jesus Christ were trustworthy witnesses.

It is Reasonable To Believe God Has Sent A Message

In a sermon entitled, "Jesus is Alive—True or False?" Lee Strobel says, "Five hundred and fifteen people—that's a lot of witnesses. I had to stop to put that into context! Think about it this way: if we were holding a trial to determine the facts concerning the resurrection, and if we were to call to the witness stand every eyewitness who personally encountered the resurrected Jesus and we cross-examined each of them for only 15 minutes, and if we went around the clock without a break, how long do you think we'd be sitting here? This first-hand eyewitness testimony would continue through tonight, through all day Sunday and Sunday night, through all day Monday and Monday night, through all day Tuesday and Tuesday night, through all day Wednesday and Wednesday night, through all day Thursday—and we'd be listening to the last eyewitness account at about 3 o'clock next Friday morning! After listening for more than 128 hours, who could walk away unconvinced? As a legal affairs journalist, I've covered scores of criminal trials, but I've never seen a case with anywhere near as much eyewitness testimony as that!"

In that sermon, Strobel also says, "Who would you guess is the most successful defense attorney in the world? F. Lee Bailey? Well, he's fallen on hard times. Johnnie Cochran? Let's check an authoritative source on this: the Guinness Book of World Records. It says on page 547: 'Most successful lawyer: Sir Lionel Luckhoo … (who) succeeded in getting his 245th successive murder charge acquittal by January 1, 1985." That's an astonishing feat that nobody in the world has come close to replicating—245 murder trials in a row, either won before a jury or on appeal. No wonder he's renowned as the real-life Perry Mason. What skills do you think he needed to rise to that unprecedented level of courtroom success? Certainly, he must be smart and savvy. He must have tremendous analytical skills so he can dissect what may appear on the surface to be an air-tight case. And he must be a world-class expert on what constitutes reliable and persuasive evidence. All of that describes Luckhoo, who was knighted twice by Queen Elizabeth and who also served as a distinguished diplomat and a justice on his country's highest court. As we approach Easter, wouldn't it be interesting to get an opinion from an expert like Luckhoo on the evidence for the resurrection of Jesus Christ? Well, we're in luck, so to speak. During his spiritual journey, Luckhoo turned his expertise to the question of whether the resurrection of Jesus Christ fits the test of legal evidence. And here's the conclusion he ultimately reached: 'I say unequivocally that the evidence for the resurrection of Jesus Christ is so overwhelming that it compels acceptance by proof which leaves absolutely no room for doubt'" (for the complete sermon, see https://sermoncentral.com/sermons/jesus-is-alive-true-or-false-lee-strobel-sermon-on-apologetics-jesus-72274? page=1).

Extra-biblical Sources Secular sources outside the Bible mentioned the resurrection of Jesus. Josephus (AD ca. 37-ca. 100), a first-century Jewish historian, wrote, "Now there was about this time Jesus, a wise man, if it be lawful to call him a man; for he was a doer of wonderful works, a teacher of such men as receive the truth with pleasure. He drew over to him both many of the Jews and many of the Gentiles. He was [the] Christ. And when Pilate, at the suggestion of the principal men amongst us, had condemned him to the cross, those that loved him at the first did not forsake him; for he appeared to them alive again the third day; as the divine prophets had foretold these and ten thousand other wonderful things concerning him. And the tribe of Christians, so named from him, are not extinct at this day" (Antiquities of the

Jews, 18, 3, 3; see a free copy of his work at https://www.gutenberg.org/files/2848/2848-h/2848-h.htm).

Scholars have debated some of these statements, namely "He was the Christ" and "He appeared to them alive again." Some argue that Josephus, being a Jew, would not have written that Jesus was the Messiah and that he was resurrected from the dead.

Paul L. Maier, Emeritus Professor of Ancient History, Western Michigan University, says explanations of the debated statements fall into three basic camps: "1. The original passage is entirely authentic—a minority position. 2. It is entirely a Christian forgery—a much smaller minority position; and 3. It contains Christian interpolations in what was Josephus's original, authentic material about Jesus—the large majority position today, particularly in view of the Agapian text ... which shows no signs of interpolation" (see the complete article at https://www.namb.net/apologetics/resource/josephus-and-jesus/; published March 30, 2016).

Maier explains, "Although this passage is so worded in the Josephus manuscripts as early as the third-century church historian Eusebius, scholars have long suspected a Christian interpolation, since Josephus could hardly have believed Jesus to be the Messiah or in his resurrection and have remained, as he did, a non-Christian Jew. In 1972, however, Professor Schlomo Pines of the Hebrew University in Jerusalem announced his discovery of a different manuscript tradition of Josephus's writings in the tenth-century Melkite historian Agapius, which reads as follows at Antiquities 18:63: "At this time, there was a wise man called Jesus, and his conduct was good, and he was known to be virtuous. Many people among the Jews and the other nations became his disciples. Pilate condemned him to be crucified and to die. But those who had become his disciples did not abandon his discipleship. They reported that he had appeared to them three days after his crucifixion and that he was alive. Accordingly, he was perhaps the Messiah, concerning whom the prophets have reported wonders. And the tribe of the Christians, so named after him, has not disappeared to this day. Here, clearly, is language that a Jew could have written without conversion to Christianity (Schlomo Pines, *An Arabic Version of the Testimonium Flavianum and its Implications* [Jerusalem: Israel Academy of Sciences and Humanities, 1971])."

Maier comments, "This, Josephus's second reference to Jesus, shows no tampering whatever with the text, and it is present in all Josephus manuscripts.... The vast majority of contemporary scholars regard this passage as genuine in its entirety, and concur with ranking Josephus expert Louis H. Feldman in his notation in the Loeb Classical Library edition of Josephus: '...few have doubted the genuineness of this passage on James' (Louis H. Feldman, tr., Josephus, IX [Cambridge, MA: Harvard University Press, 1965], 496)." Maier adds, "Moreover, Jesus is portrayed as a 'wise man' come [sophos aner], a phrase not used by Christians but employed by Josephus for such personalities as David and Solomon in the Hebrew Bible."

Other secular sources include Tacitus (AD 56-ca. 120), a Roman historian, renowned for his works The Annals and The Histories. He mentions Christians and refers to the execution of Jesus during the reign of Tiberius. Lucian of Samosata (AD ca. 125-after 180), a Greek satirist, wrote The Death of Peregrine, which includes a satirical portrayal of Christians and their beliefs. He was critical of Christianity, but his work confirms the existence of Jesus as a historical figure. Mara bar-Serapion, a Syrian philosopher who wrote a letter to his son from prison after

AD 73. The letter includes a comparison between Socrates, Pythagoras, and a "wise King" who was killed by the Jews, which is widely interpreted as a reference to Jesus. These historians provide historical perspectives on the rise of Christianity. Their writings corroborate Christian sources.

The evidence for the resurrection of Jesus Christ is convincing. Based on what we know, it is reasonable to believe that Jesus rose from the dead. Even atheists have been convinced. For example, see Lee Strobel's book, The *Case for Christ*, and Warner J. Wallace's book, *Cold-Case Christianity*.

Frank Morison, an investigative journalist, set out to disprove the Christian faith by showing Christ's resurrection as a farce. As a result of his investigation, Morison became a Christian and wrote the book *Who Moved the Stone?* (1930).

Personal Experience

In the 2,000 years since Christ died and rose from the dead, millions upon millions of people have testified that they have believed in Jesus Christ and have the assurance of eternal life. For example, Paul said, "I know whom I have believed and am persuaded that He is able to keep what I have committed to Him until that Day" (2 Tim. 1:12). Paul knew whom (not "what") he had trusted. Moreover, he was persuaded that this Person was able to keep him. He was absolutely convinced (Kent). The Greek word translated "keep" means "to guard, preserve." The picture is that God is the Trustee. Paul has deposited himself into the safekeeping of the Trustee, who is able to "guard the deposit" of Paul's "temporal and eternal welfare" (Hiebert; see also Calvin, Alford, Hendriksen, and Kent). "That day" is a reference to the

Judgment Seat of Christ, when Paul will "receive his reward for his gospel labors" (Hiebert). As the song says:

> I know not why God's wondrous grace to me He hath made known,
> Nor why, unworthy Christ in love redeemed me for His own.
>> Chorus: But "I know whom I have believed, and am persuaded that He is able to keep that which I've committed unto Him against that Day."
>
> I know not how this saving faith to me He did impart
> Nor how believing in His Word wrought peace within my heart.
>> Chorus: But "I know whom I have believed, and am persuaded that He is able to keep that which I've committed unto Him against that Day."

Granted, personal experience is not proof. People can claim they have experienced all kinds of things, but that doesn't prove that their experience was real. They could have been hallucinating. On the other hand, if Jesus rose from the dead and promised eternal life to those who believed in Him, it is reasonable to expect that people would experience that, and if they didn't, it would cause people to doubt whether or not the whole thing was true. So, personal experience has value in this case.

Summary: The reasons for believing that God has given us a message in the Bible are fulfilled prophecy, the resurrection of Jesus Christ, and the personal experience of those who have trusted Christ for the gift of eternal life.

It is Reasonable To Believe God Has Sent A Message

If you believe that Jesus Christ is God in the flesh, who died in your place to pay for your sins and who rose from the dead, you can not only know there is a God, but you can also know Him personally by trusting His Son for the gift of eternal life. The question is, "Will you trust Jesus Christ?"

Atheists get converted. Perhaps the most well-known example is C. S. Lewis, an atheist who was a professor at Oxford University and Cambridge University. Madelyn Murray O'Hair successfully removed prayer from public schools, using her son Bill as a test case. As an adult, Bill became a Christian. As a philosophy major in college, John Warwick Montgomery investigated the claims of Christianity "to preserve intellectual integrity." As a result, he was converted and became a renowned Christian Apologist and Lutheran theologian. Lee Strobel, who has a Law degree from Yale, was an avowed atheist. As a result of his wife's conversion, he began investigating the biblical claims about Christ and became a Christian.

Chapter 4

It Is Reasonable To Believe God's Message Is Accurate: Part 1

Even assuming the Bible is God's message to us, there are still questions that remain. Are there books in the Bible that should not be there? Are there "lost books" that ought to be in the Bible but did not make it? How was the Bible put together? Who determined which books to include and which books to exclude?

This chapter is a condensed version of my book, *The Formation of the Bible*. It is available at Amazon and Barnes & Noble, and at a discount on my website at www.insightsfromtheword.com.

Theologians refer to this issue as the "canon." The English word "canon" comes from a Greek word that originally meant "rod, bar, measuring rule," hence, "a rule or standard." Theologically, it refers to a collection of books that meet the standard of being the Word of God.

The Bible was written over about fifteen hundred years. The process began with Moses; later, other books were added to the canon. Therefore, the questions in forming the Bible are: "When were the additional books added? Who decides what books should be part of the collection of inspired books? The ultimate issue is, "When was the collection of inspired books (the canon) closed?"

The Formation of the Old Testament

There is no record, either within or outside the Bible, concerning the formation of the Hebrew Bible (the Protestant Old Testament). Unger states, "Precisely when or how the entire group of Old Testament books was set apart and definitely recognized as the Word of God is veiled in obscurity" (Unger, p. 73). Nevertheless, based on what the Bible says, it is possible to construct a plausible scenario of how the Old Testament was formed.

Biblical Data
The Writings of Moses The formation of the Old Testament begins with the writings of Moses. Note the threefold process.

1. God spoke. God spoke to Moses. The words "God said" occur ten times in the first chapter of Genesis. The same thing is recorded in the other four books Moses wrote (Ex. 6:2; 20:1; Lev. 1:1; Num. 1:1; Deut. 2:2; etc.).

2. Moses wrote. At God's direction, Moses wrote the words of God. "So Moses came and told the people all the words of the LORD and all the judgments. And all the people answered with one voice and said, 'All the words which the LORD has said we will do.' And Moses wrote all the words of the LORD. And he rose early in the morning and built an altar at the foot of the mountain, and twelve pillars according to the twelve tribes of Israel" (Ex. 24:3-4; see also Ex. 17:14, 34:27; Deut. 17:18, 27:3). Moses wrote the words (plural) of the Lord. As an example, notice how often in the book of Numbers, Moses says he is writing what God said (Num. 1:1; 2:1; 3:5; 4:1; 5:1; 5:5; 6:1; 7:4; 8:1; 9:1; 10:1; 11:16; 12:5-6; 13:1; 14:11; 14:20; 15:1; 16:20; 17:1; 18:1; 19:1; 20:7; 21:8; 22:9; etc.).

3. People took note. God saw to it that people took note that what Moses wrote was the words of God (Josh. 1:7-8). God worked so that His words to Moses were preserved, recognized, and used as the Word of God.

The Word of God, written by Moses, was preserved. "So it was, when Moses had completed writing the words of this law in a book when they were finished, that Moses commanded the Levites, who bore the ark of the covenant of the Lord, saying, 'Take this Book of the Law, and put it beside the ark of the covenant of the Lord your God, that it may be there as a witness against you'" (Deut. 31:24-26; 31:9-11). Moses wrote the Word of God in a book, which was placed beside the Ark of the Covenant. Thus, the Word of God given to Moses was preserved.

The Word of God, written by Moses, was recognized as the Word of God. Moses said, "And it shall be, on the day when you cross over the Jordan to the land which the LORD your God is giving you, that you shall set up for yourselves large stones, and whitewash them with lime. You shall write on them all the words of this law, when you have crossed over, that you may enter the land which the LORD your God is giving you, 'a land flowing with milk and honey,' just as the LORD God of your fathers promised you. Therefore, it shall be when you have crossed over the Jordan, that on Mount Ebal you shall set up these stones, which I command you today, and you shall whitewash them with lime" (Deut. 27:2-4). When the children of Israel arrived in the land, they did as Moses instructed so that the people of God acknowledged the Word of God (Josh. 8:30-35).

The Word of God, written by Moses, was used as the Word of God. What Moses wrote was not preserved in a museum to satisfy people's curiosity. It was preserved for use. When Moses died, God told his successor, Joshua, to hear and heed what Moses wrote: "Only be strong and very courageous, that you may observe to do according to all the law which Moses My servant commanded you; do not turn from it to the right hand or to the left, that you may prosper wherever you go. This Book of the Law shall not depart from your mouth, but you shall meditate in it day and night, that you may observe to do according to all that is written in it. For then you will make your way prosperous, and then you will have good success" (Josh. 1:7-8). God spoke of the "book" of the Law. The five books of Moses were considered one book of "the Law." The book of the Law was to be thought about, talked about, and obeyed. The written Word of God was to be used.

As Moses had instructed, Joshua made the Word of God available to the people. "Now Joshua built an altar to the LORD God of Israel in Mount Ebal, as Moses the servant of the LORD had commanded the children of Israel, as it is written in the Book of the Law of Moses: 'an altar of whole stones over which no man has wielded an iron tool.' And they offered burnt offerings to the LORD on it and sacrificed peace offerings. And there, in the presence of the children of Israel, he wrote on the stones a copy of the law of Moses, which he had written. Then all Israel, with their elders and officers and judges, stood on either side of the ark before the priests, the Levites, who bore the ark of the covenant of the LORD, the stranger as well as he who was born among them. Half of them were in front of Mount Gerizim and half of them in front of Mount Ebal, as Moses, the servant of the LORD had commanded before, that they should bless the people of Israel. And afterward he read all the words of the law, the blessings and the cursings, according to all that is written in the Book of the Law. There was not a word of all that Moses had commanded which Joshua did not read before all the assembly of Israel, with the women, the little ones, and the strangers who were living among them" (Josh. 8:30-35).

There is a question as to how much of the Law was written on stone. Some suggest that Joshua wrote the Ten Commandments (Woudstra). Others believe that what he wrote was the blessings and curses of Deuteronomy 27 and 28 (Bush). The Jews believed that what was written was the 613 commandments of the Pentateuch (see Woudstra). Still others have concluded that it was the whole book of Deuteronomy.

It is possible that all five books of Moses were written on stone. Archeologists have discovered inscribed pillars from six to eight feet in height in the Middle East. Some of these inscriptions were three times the length of the book of Deuteronomy (Campbell). Later in history, daily "newspapers" were chiseled in stone six feet high and three feet wide. Tourists today can see examples of such stone newspapers in the ruins of ancient Ephesus.

Note the process: God spoke. Moses wrote what God said. The written Word of God was preserved (Deut. 31:24-26), was to be recognized as the Word of God (Deut. 27:2-4), and was to be used as the Word of God (Deut. 17:18-20). The people noted that what was written was the Word of God (Josh. 1:7-8; 8:30-35).

From the very beginning of the written Word of God and throughout Israel's history, the Law was recognized and regarded as the Word of God. The Law of Moses was to be written in a book for the king (Deut. 17:18-20). Joshua was to meditate on "the book of the Law," talk about it, and obey it (Jos. 1:7-8). The Law was put on public display (Josh. 8:30-35; see also "book of the Law of Moses" in Josh. 23:6). David charged Solomon to obey the commandment of the Lord "as it is written in the Law of

Moses" (1 Kings 2:1-3). Amaziah "executed his servants who had murdered his father the king, but the children of the murderers he did not execute, according to what is written in the Book of the Law of Moses, in which the LORD commanded, saying, 'Fathers shall not be put to death for their children, nor shall children be put to death for their fathers; but a person shall be put to death for his own sin'" (2 Kings 14:5-6; 21:8). In the days of Josiah the "Book of the Law" was recognized as the Word of God (2 Kings 22:8-23:1-2). After the rebuilding of the Temple, "They assigned the priests to their divisions and the Levites to their divisions, over the service of God in Jerusalem, as it is written in the Book of Moses" (Ezra 6:18). After the return from exile, Ezra read "the Book of the Law" publicly (Neh. 8:1-5). Nehemiah read "from the Book of Moses in the hearing of the people (Neh. 13:1). Malachi wrote, "Remember the Law of Moses, My servant, Which I commanded him in Horeb for all Israel, With the statutes and judgments" (Mal. 4:4). All were to meditate in the Law of the Lord (Ps. 1:2). From the time of Moses to the end of the history of Israel in the Old Testament, the Law was called a "book" (Deut. 17:18-20; Jos. 1:7-8; Neh. 8:1-5).

Thus, the book of Moses established a "canon," a collection of books recognized as the Word of God (Josh. 1:7-8; 8:30-35). With his writings, the "Bible" was born. The writing of Moses furnished a foundation for all subsequent writings and supplied the concept of canonicity (see R. K. Harrison, p. 265).

The Writings of Other Authors As other authors wrote, again, there was a threefold process.

1. God spoke. Many Others in ancient Israel claimed God spoke to them (Isa. 1:1-2; Jer. 1:1-4; Ezek. 1:1-3; 32:1-3; Hosea 1:1; Joel 1:1; Amos 1:1-3; Obad. 1; Jonah 1:1; Micah 1:1; Nahum

1:1, 12; Hab. 1:1; 2:1-2; Zeph. 1:1; Haggai 1:1; Zech. 1:1; 1:4-6; Mal. 1:1). The Old Testament explicitly says God spoke through prophets: "Yes, they made their hearts like flint, refusing to hear the law and the words which the LORD of hosts had sent by His Spirit through the former prophets. Thus great wrath came from the LORD of hosts" (Zech. 7:12). Many parts of the Old Testament claim to be the Word of God. It is said that such expressions as "the Lord said," "the Lord spoke," and "the Word of the Lord came" are found 3,808 times in the Old Testament. The New Testament says, "For prophecy never came by the will of man, but holy men of God spoke as they were moved by the Holy Spirit" (2 Pet. 1:21).

2. Men wrote. Those to whom God spoke ("moved") wrote the Word of God given to them (see the long list of references in the previous paragraph!). First Samuel says Samuel "wrote it in a book and laid it up before the LORD" (1 Sam. 10:25). Keil and Delitzsch say, "It was no doubt placed in the tabernacle, where the Law of Moses was also deposited, by the side of the fundamental law of the divine state in Israel." As Gill points out, in the Tabernacle, it would be accessible, at least by a priest, safe, and preserved for future use.

3. People took note. People took note that what these authors wrote was the written Word of God, and they used it as the Word of God (Zech. 7:12). In other words, the Old Testament began with the writings of Moses, and as other inspired writings were produced, God saw to it that they were recognized as His Word.

For example, Isaiah quotes Micah (*cf.* Micah 4:1-3 with Isaiah 2:2-4). Keil says Micah wrote first and Delitzsch proves that in his commentary on Isaiah (Micah wrote between 735 and 710 BC; Isaiah wrote in 680 BC).

Is It Reasonable To Believe There Is A God?

The elders of Jeremiah's day quote Micah. Jeremiah records, "Then certain of the elders of the land rose up and spoke to all the assembly of the people, saying: 'Micah of Moresheth prophesied in the days of Hezekiah king of Judah, and spoke to all the people of Judah, saying, 'Thus says the LORD of hosts: 'Zion shall be plowed like a field, Jerusalem shall become heaps of ruins, And the mountain of the temple like the bare hills of the forest'" (Jer. 26:17-18). In Jeremiah 26:18, the elders quote Micah 3:12 as an inspired utterance of the Lord. Micah prophesied in the days of Hezekiah, who reigned from 715-686 BC. These elders lived in the days of Jehoiakim (Jer. 26:1), who reigned from 609-598 BC! In other words, they are quoting Micah, who preached about a hundred years before, which indicates that they must be quoting what Micah wrote. Laetsch says, "One hundred years after Micah had spoken, these elders were able to quote the text that has come down to us verbatim. A remarkable testimony for the general accuracy of the copies current among the people and handed down through the centuries!" (Laetsch, p. 221). Thompson says, "The quotation of Mic. 3:12 shows that the oracles of the prophets were preserved and were well known" (Thompson, p. 527). The elders acknowledged that what Micah had written one hundred years before was the Word of God.

Jeremiah wrote what he was commanded to write and Daniel recognized that what Jeremiah wrote was the Word of God. Jeremiah wrote, "Now it came to pass in the fourth year of Jehoiakim the son of Josiah, king of Judah, that this word came to Jeremiah from the LORD, saying: 'Take a scroll of a book and write on it all the words that I have spoken to you against Israel, against Judah, and against all the nations, from the day I spoke to you, from the days of Josiah even to this day'" (Jer. 36:1-2). One of the things Jeremiah prophesied was that the captivity would last seventy years (Jer. 25:8-12; 29:10; Dan. 9:2). The seventy years began when Nebuchadnezzar conquered Jerusalem (Jer. 25:8-12), which began in 605 BC. Seventy years later, Daniel said, "In the first year of his reign I, Daniel, understood by the books the number of the years specified by the word of the Lord, given through Jeremiah the prophet, that He would accomplish seventy years in the desolations of Jerusalem" (Dan. 9:2). Daniel was reading "the books," when he found "the word of the LORD through Jeremiah the prophet." Some say that the article ("the") "does not denote a collection of known sacred writings in which the writings of Jeremiah were included" (Keil). Others claim that the article likely indicates a "collection, recognized as sacred" (Wood). Baldwin says, it indicates "prophetic books were considered canonical at the time of writing." Seventy years after Jeremiah wrote, Daniel acknowledged that what he wrote was the Word of God.

Unger argues that passages such as Nehemiah 9:26-31, Zechariah 1:4, 7:7, 7:12, and Malachi 3:7 "demonstrate that the words of the prophets were believed to have had the same divine sanction as the Mosaic Law" because "a similar divine penalty was meted out upon the transgression of the one as of the other" (Unger, p. 61). Ryrie says, "The prophets claimed to be speaking the Word of God, and their prophecies were recognized as authoritative. Notice these references: Joshua 6:26 compared with 1 Kings 16:34; Joshua 24:29-33 compared with Judges 2:8-9; 2 Chronicles 36:22-23 compared with Ezra 1:1-4; Daniel 9:2 compared with Jeremiah 25:11-12" (Ryrie, p. 106).

Note the process: God spoke. Men wrote what God said. People took note that what they wrote was the Word of God.

To sum up, the formation of the Bible began with the writings of Moses, and as God inspired other books, He ensured that they were recognized, preserved, and used as His Word.

The Old Testament is not just a collection of all the books written in ancient Israel. Other books were written that did not become part of the Old Testament. For example, 1 Chronicles says, "Now the acts of King David, first and last, indeed they are written in the book of Samuel, the seer, in the book of Nathan the prophet, and in the book of Gad, the seer" (1 Chron. 29:29; see Unger, p. 52 for a list of others). These were books written by prophets. What they wrote might have been true, but God did not inspire them to be part of His Word.

Moreover, the people were warned not to add anything to what God said. "You shall not add to the word which I command you, nor take from it, that you may keep the commandments of the LORD your God which I command you" (Deut. 4:2). "Whatever I command you, be careful to observe it; you shall not add to it nor take away from it" (Deut. 12:32). "Every word of God is pure; He is a shield to those who put their trust in Him. Do not add to His words, Lest He rebuke you, and you be found a liar" (Prov. 30:5-6). Such statements "reminded the Jews of the sacredness of that inspired text" (McDonald, p. 75).

Therefore, if God inspired some books and not others, and if He warned His people not to add to His Word, it is reasonable to believe that He providentially worked to ensure that His books were collected. Many scholars have reached the same conclusions.

Young says, "In His good providence, God brought it about that His people should recognize and receive His Word. How He planted this conviction in their hearts with respect to the identity of His Word, we may not be able fully to understand or explain"

(Young, p. 168).

Unger observes, "It would be highly unreasonable to suppose that God, who deigned to reveal Himself to man and so overshadowed and worked upon man that he might receive and record the revelation inerrantly, would not continue to exert His power providentially in preserving the precious documents from destruction and in guiding in their eventual collection and arrangement as a complete and authoritative whole" (Unger, pp. 46-47).

Archer says, "The Biblical authors indicate very clearly, whenever the matter comes up, that the various books of the Bible were canonical from the moment of their inception, by virtue of the divine authority ('Thus saith the Lord') behind them, and the books received immediate recognition and acceptance by the faithful as soon as they were made aware of the writings" (Archer, p. 71). Archer argues that it was simply a matter of recognition of the quality inherent in the inspired books. He illustrates: "When a child recognizes his own parents from a multitude of other adults, he does not impart any new quality of parenthood by such an act; he simply recognizes a relationship which already exists. So also with a list of authoritative books drawn up by ecclesiastical synods or councils. They did not impart canonicity to a single page of Scripture; they simply acknowledged the divine inspiration of religious documents which were inherently canonical from the time they were first composed and formally rejected other books for which canonicity had been falsely claimed" (Archer, pp. 69-70).

Harrison says, "The Spirit of God that inspired these compositions also worked in the hearts and minds of the chosen people to testify to them that the writings were in fact the divine

Word. It was this witness, in conjunction with the conscious human response, that was evidently the ultimate determining agent in the formulation of the canon. Had the question of canonicity merely rested upon purely academic decisions without an acknowledged concept of inspiration, it is impossible to see how the Jews could ever have come to accept the Old Testament books as being of divine authority" (R. K. Harrison, p. 284).

Extra Biblical Data

There are indications of a Jewish canon outside the Old Testament. The book of Sirach, also known as Ecclesiasticus (ca. 190 BC), speaks of the "Law of the Most High" (Sirach 39:1). It also says, "It was Ezekiel who saw the glorious vision, which was shown him upon the chariot of the cherubim. For he made mention of the enemies under the figure of the rain, and directed those who went right. And of the twelve prophets let the memorial be blessed, and let their bones flourish again out of their place: for they comforted Jacob, and delivered them by assured hope" (Sirach 49:8-10).

McDonald says, "This passage is in the heart of Sirach's celebrated 'history of famous men,' which illustrates significant familiarity with the Law and Prophets, which begins in Sir. 44:1 with the words, 'Let us now sing the praises of famous men, our ancestors in their generations.' Sirach shows an awareness of the books of Joshua (46:1-6), Samuel (46:13-47:11), and Kings (47:12-49:3) as well as several other well-known names in the OT writings: Isaiah (48:20-25), Jeremiah (49:6-7), Ezekiel (49:8), and the Twelve Prophets (49:10). His reference to the 'Twelve Prophets' suggests that by the time that Sirach wrote (180 B.C.E), all of the Minor Prophets were collected in one scroll. The entire passage, Sir. 44:1-49:10 suggests that the heroes described in these prophetic writings were familiar to the Jews, that they probably were widely acknowledged in a scriptural or authoritative manner, and that their authors were viewed as spokespersons for God. Sirach does not introduce these famous persons (except for Elijah [48:10]) but assumes widespread knowledge of them. His purpose was not to celebrate their writings but to celebrate their lives. Whether their writings were identified as Scripture is not obvious, but Sirach's knowledge of them is at least suggestive of their authoritative role in the Judaism of his day" (McDonald, pp. 82-83).

The Prologue to Sirach (ca. 130 BC) was written by the grandson of Sirach, who translated his grandfather's work into Greek and added a prologue. The Prologue says, "Many great teachings have been given to us through the Law and the prophets and the others that followed them, and for these, we should praise Israel for instruction and wisdom. Now, those who read the scriptures must not only themselves understand them but must also, as lovers of learning, be able through the spoken and written word to help the outsiders. So my grandfather Jesus, who had devoted himself, especially to the reading of the Law and the prophets and the other books of our ancestors, and had acquired considerable proficiency in them, was himself also led to write something pertaining to instruction and wisdom so that by becoming familiar also with his book those who love learning might make even greater progress in living according to the law." This is the oldest known reference to a threefold division of the Old Testament, comprising the Law, the Prophets, and other books (Archer, pp. 62-63; R. K. Harrison, p. 270). The threefold division indicates a canon.

Second Maccabees (ca. 124 BC) says, "The same things are reported in the records and in the memoirs of Nehemiah, and also that he founded a library and collected the books about the kings and prophets, and the writings of David, and letters of kings about votive offerings. In the same way, Judas [Maccabeus] also collected all the books that had been lost on account of the war that had come upon us, and they are in our possession. So if you have need of them, send people to get them for you" (2 Macc. 2:13-15). McDonald explains, "This tradition claims that Nehemiah collected books for a library comprising the books of the 'kings' (1-2 Samuel and 1-2 Kings?), the 'prophets,' and the 'writings of David' (the psalms?)" (McDonald, p. 85). Surely, his collection included the Law (Neh. 8:1-5; 13:1).

The Dead Sea Scrolls may serve as an indication of the Old Testament canon. Ryrie points out that "about 175 of the 500 Dead Sea scrolls are biblical. There are several copies of many of the books of the Old Testament, and all the Old Testament books are represented among the scrolls, except Esther. The existence of biblical books among the scrolls does not in itself prove their canonicity since some of the non-canonical books are also present. However, many of the Dead Sea Scrolls are commentaries, and so far, all of those commentaries deal only with canonical books. That seems to show that a distinction between canonical and non-canonical books was recognized. Also, twenty of the thirty-nine books of the Old Testament are quoted or referred to as Scripture. In summary, the scrolls give positive evidence for the canonicity of all but Chronicles, Esther, and the Song of Solomon" (Ryrie, pp. 106-107). Additionally, a quotation from one of the scrolls suggests a threefold division (see McDonald, pp. 90-93; his point is that the individual books are not mentioned).

Around AD 40, Philo refers to the same threefold division (Contemplative Life, II, 475), and so does Josephus (AD 37-100,

Against Apion, 1:8, quoted below).

The Final Formation of the Old Testament

There is no record of the final formation of the Old Testament into a single volume. Based on what the Old Testament says, it is reasonable to believe that when God ceased speaking, the formation of the canon also ceased. There are indications that happened.

The Promise in Malachi Malachi concludes his book with a promise of a prophet who will come just before the Day of the Lord (Mal. 4:5). Ryrie says, "In Malachi 4:5, there is an indication that the prophetic witness would end with Malachi and not begin again until the coming of an Elijah-type prophet in the person of John the Baptist (Matt. 17: 11-12)" (Ryrie, p. 106).

A Comment in 1 Maccabees The Apocryphal book of 1 Maccabees (ca. 100 BC) says, "There was great distress in Israel, such as has not been since the time the prophets ceased to appear among them" (1 Maccabees 9:27). In other words, about 100 BC it was recognized that God had not sent a prophet to Israel in some time, which implies that no more Scripture had been written.

The Statements by Josephus Josephus (AD 37-95) writes, "For we have not an innumerable multitude of books among us, disagreeing from and contradicting one another [as the Greeks have], but only twenty-two books, which contain the records of all the past times; which are justly believed to be divine; and of them five belong to Moses, which contain his laws and the traditions of the origin of mankind till his death. This interval of time was a little short of three thousand years, but as to the time from the death of Moses till the reign of Artaxerxes, king of Persia, who reigned after Xerxes, the prophets, who were after Moses, wrote down what was done in their times in thirteen books. The remaining four books contain hymns to God and precepts for the conduct of human life. It is true, our history hath been written since Artaxerxes very particularly, but hath not been esteemed of the like authority with the former by our forefathers, because there hath not been an exact succession of prophets since that time; and how firmly we have given credit to those books of our own nation, is evident by what we do; for during so many ages as have already passed, no one has been so bold as either to add anything to them, to take anything from them, or to make any change in them; but it becomes natural to all Jews, immediately and from their very birth, to esteem those books to contain divine doctrines, and to persist in them, and, if occasion be, willingly to die for them. For it is no new thing for our captives, many of them in number, and frequently in time, to be seen to endure racks and deaths of all kinds upon the theatres, that they may not be obliged to say one word against our laws and the records that contain them; whereas there are none at all among the Greeks who would undergo the least harm on that account, no, nor in case all the writings that are among them were to be destroyed; for they take them to be such discourses as are famed agreeably to the inclinations of those that write them; and they have justly the same opinion of the ancient writers, since they see some of the present generation bold enough to write about such affairs, wherein they were not present, nor had concern enough to inform themselves about them from those that knew them: examples of which may be had in this late war of ours, where some persons have written histories, and published them, without having been in the places concerned, or having been near them when the actions were done; but these men put a few things together by hearsay, and insolently abuse the world, and call these writings by the name of Histories" (Josephus, Against Apion, 1:8).

According to Josephus, a first-century Jew, the Jews had twenty-two books they believed to be divine. He says those twenty-two books consisted of the five books of Moses, thirteen from the prophets, and four containing "hymns to God, and precepts for the conduct of human life." The question is, "How does the twenty-two-book canon of Josephus compare to the Hebrew Bible and the Protestant Old Testament?"

The Hebrew Bible contains twenty-four books, beginning with Genesis and ending with 2 Chronicles (see the traditional Masoretic text). Does that mean that the Hebrew Bible contains two more books than the list of Josephus? No. It has been suggested that Josephus arrived at twenty-two books by combining Ruth with Judges and Lamentations with Jeremiah (Bruce, CS, p. 33). Origen noted that the Hebrew alphabet consists of twenty-two letters (Unger, p. 55).

The Protestant Old Testament has thirty-nine books. Does that mean it has more books than Josephus? No. Following the Septuagint, the Greek translation of the Hebrew Bible (250-160 BC), the Protestant Bible divides the books of Samuel, Kings, Chronicles, and Ezra-Nehemiah into two books each (making eight instead of four). It divides the Twelve Minor Prophets into individual books (making twelve instead of one). Thus, fifteen additional books (4+11=15) appear to be added, but there is no further material, only a different division (Unger, p. 54). The arrangement is also different. The Hebrew Bible begins with Genesis and closes with 2 Chronicles. The Protestant Old Testament begins with Genesis and ends with Malachi, but its content is identical to that of the Hebrew Bible. Thus, the twenty-four-book division of the Hebrew Bible is identical to the thirty-nine-book division of the Protestant Old Testament. The only difference is the division and the order (Unger, p. 54).

In other words, the twenty-two-book division of Josephus is identical to the twenty-four-book division of the Masoretic text, which is the same as the thirty-nine-book division of the Protestant Old Testament. Josephus speaks of a threefold division consisting of the Law, the Prophets, and Hymns.

According to Josephus, anything written after Artaxerxes has not been esteemed with the same authority as the former divine works because there has not been an "exact succession of prophets since that time." He clearly says, "No one has been so bold as either to add anything to them, to take anything from them, or to make any change in them; but it becomes natural to all Jews, immediately and from their very birth to esteem, those books to contain divine doctrines, and to persist in them, and, if occasion be, willingly to die for them." He adds that this is unlike anything non-Jews would do.

Later, a rabbinic tradition claimed, "When the latter prophets died, that is, Haggai, Zechariah, and Malachi, then the Holy Spirit came to an end in Israel" (Sotah 13:2, Neusner, Tosefta, 885, cited by McDonald, p. 419).

Bruce observes that Josephus does not mean the gift of prophecy died out because he mentions its exercise among the Essenes (Josephus, Antiquities, 13:311, 15.373-379), by John Hycanus (134-104 BC; Josephus, 13:300), and he even claims to have had the gift himself (Josephus, Jewish Wars 3:351-354; Bruce, CS, p. 33). As Archer explains, Josephus says, "No more canonical writings have been composed since the reign of Artaxerxes, son of Xerxes (464-424 B.C.), i.e., since the time of Malachi." Furthermore, "No additional material was ever included in the canonical twenty-two books during the centuries between (i.e., from 424 B. C. to AD 90)" (Archer, p. 64).

In other words, based on what Josephus wrote, the content of the Hebrew Bible, the threefold division of the Hebrew Bible, and his statement about the cessation of prophets indicate there was a final formation of the Old Testament canon since Artaxerxes, whose dates are 465-425 BC (Unger, p. 71).

To sum up, there is no record of a final formation of the Old Testament into a single volume, but the promise of Malachi implies there would be no more prophets until the arrival of a prophet before the Day of the Lord, and Josephus indicates that there were no more prophets after the time of Artaxerxes. Thus, it is reasonable to believe that the formation of the Old Testament canon stopped when God stopped speaking.

Confirmation

While there is no biblical or historical record of a formal recognition of the Old Testament, there is confirmation that a closed canon existed in the first century.

Names in the New Testament The New Testament uses names for the Old Testament that seem to be referring to "the whole Old Testament" (Thiessen, p. 4), such as "the Scripture" (2 Tim. 3:16; 1 Pet. 2:6) and "the Holy Scriptures" (Rom. 1:2). Jesus calls Psalm 118:22 Scripture (Mt. 21:42). He speaks of "the Scripture" as if there was a collection of books (Mt. 22:29; Lk. 24:32; Jn. 5:39; 10:35). Harrison says, "By the time of Christ, it would seem, the Old Testament existed as a complete collection. The evidence presented by the New Testament writers indicates that the Old Testament as a whole was referred to as 'the Scriptures' or 'the Scripture' at that period to designate a familiar and unified group of inspired and authoritative writings" (R. K. Harrison, p. 276). "The very word Scripture, as it is used in the New Testament, carries the idea of canonicity, or that which measures up to the divine standard, that which is the authoritative word of God (Baker, p. 76).

Not only is the term "Scripture" used in the New Testament of the whole Old Testament, so is the term "law." Jesus says, "It is written in your law" and quotes Psalm 82:6 (Jn. 10:34). Harrison says the term "law" in John 10:34 refers to the "entire corpus of the Hebrew Scriptures" (R. K. Harrison, p. 265). Paul says, "In the law it is written" (1 Cor. 14:21) and cites Isaiah 28:11-12.

In addition, the expression "the Law and the Prophets" is used of the Old Testament (Mt. 5:17; 7:12; 22:40; Lk. 16:16; 24:27; Acts 13:15; 24:14; 28:23; Rom. 3:21). The Law is, of course, the Law of Moses (Jn. 10:34). The contents of "the Prophets" is never delineated in the Bible, but books in the third division are said to be from the Prophets (Mt. 24:15) and books in the third division are treated as Scripture (Acts 1:16, 2:25-31, 34-36). By using the expression "the Law and the Prophets," Paul certainly seems to be saying that he had the same Scriptures as the Jews (Acts 24:14). In the second century AD, the term "Prophets" is used of the entire Old Testament (McDonald, p. 111, who cites Justin, 1 Apol. 67). As McDonald says, "Since both Jews and Christians believed that God had inspired all Scripture, all of it was prophetic" (McDonald, p. 111).

Harrison says, "Usually the New Testament writers only mentioned the first two sections (Matt. 5:17; Lk. 16:16), but quite obviously they included the Hagiographa with the Prophets just as the Talmudic teachers did (due perhaps to the lack of a current technical term for the Hagiographa)" (R. K. Harrison, p. 269;

Hagiographa, also called Writings, consist of Psalms, Proverbs, Job, the Song of Solomon, Ruth, Lamentations, Ecclesiastes, Esther, Daniel, Ezra, Nehemiah, and Chronicles).

Ryrie agrees, "This twofold division covers all of the Old Testament" (Ryrie, p. 107). Harrison also points out, "New Testament authors commonly alluded to the Scriptures in terms of two categories—the Law and the Prophets. Support for this position has been provided by the discoveries from Qumran, where in four instances, *The Community Rule* or *Manual of Discipline* (lQS, 1:3; VIII:13 ff.) and the Zadokite Fragment (CDC, V:21; VII:15 ff.) referred to the Old Testament writings in precisely the same two categories" (R. K. Harrison, p. 276).

Even McDonald, who does not believe that the Old Testament canon was closed in the first century, says the expression "the Law and the Prophets" appears "to comprise all of the sacred Scriptures" and "sometimes the whole of the sacred writings is referred to simply as 'law'" (McDonald, p. 99)! In his commentary on Acts 28:23, Bruce states that the expression "the Law of Moses and the prophets" indicates that "his text was the whole volume of what we now call the Old Testament."

Thus, the New Testament employs a diverse range of expressions and terms to refer to the Word of God, including "Scripture," "Law," and "the Law and the prophets," among others. In other words, when the New Testament records an expression like "the Scripture says," it is the same as someone saying today, "The Bible says." Furthermore, the New Testament claims the Old Testament is the Word of God (2 Tim. 14-16; Heb. 1:1; 2 Pet. 1:20-21).

Statements by Jesus When Jesus said, "Therefore, whatever you want men to do to you, do also to them, for this is the Law and the Prophets" (Mt. 7:12), He obviously meant that the Golden Rule is the sum of the complete Old Testament (Bruce, CS, p. 32).

Jesus mentions the first and last books of the Old Testament. In condemning the religious leaders, He charged them with being guilty of shedding the blood of all the righteous from Abel to Zechariah (Mt. 23:35; Lk. 11:51). The murder of Abel is recorded in Genesis 4, and the murder of Zechariah in 2 Chronicles 24:20-21. Genesis is the first book, and 2 Chronicles is the last book in the Hebrew Bible. So the Lord says, "From the first to the last murder in the Old Testament." Thus, the Hebrew canon was complete by the time of Jesus (Bruce, CS, p. 31). Unger says this can "only have meaning if the final order and arrangement of the Hebrew canon is referred to" (Unger, p. 71).

Luke 24 says, "Beginning at Moses and all the Prophets, He (Jesus) expounded to them in all the Scriptures the things concerning Himself" (Lk. 24:27). The expression "all the prophets" added to the Law of Moses indicates a closed collection of Scriptures.

Later in Luke 24, Jesus said, "All things must be fulfilled which were written in the Law of Moses and the Prophets and the Psalms concerning Me" (Lk. 24:44). This threefold division of the Old Testament is "used in direct parallel with the phrase 'Moses and the prophets' earlier in the chapter" (Geisler, p. 367). Leiman contends that "Psalms" represents the third division of the Hebrew Bible because it stands first in some Hebrew manuscripts (Leiman, p. 40; see also Ellis, p. 9, fn 30). Beckwith says "Psalms" refers to the third part of the Hebrew canon in the Talmudic literature (Beckwith, p. 438). He also says that since Jesus cites the book of Daniel (Dan. 4:26 in Mt. 4:17; Dan. 9:27; 11:31; 12:11 in Mt. 24:15; and Dan. 7:13 in Mk. 14:62), which was a part of the

Writings, He intended the whole of the Writings when He mentioned the "Psalms" in Luke 24:44 (Beckwith, pp. 111-112).

Harrison says, "The threefold division of the canon was well established in the early Christian era. The New Testament makes it clear that the canon familiar to Jesus Christ was identical to the one that exists today. None of the Apocrypha or Pseudepigrapha is ever cited by name, much less accorded the status of Scripture, whereas Daniel is specifically quoted as a prophetic composition in Matthew 24:15. The three chief divisions were enumerated in Luke 24:44 as the Law, the Prophets, and the Psalms" (R. K. Harrison, p. 269).

To sum up, there is no record of any "formal recognition" of the Old Testament, but the references to the Old Testament in the New Testament confirm that the canon of the Old Testament was closed in the first century.

The Debate about the Old Testament

There is a debate over the canon of the Old Testament to this very day. There are books written after the close of the Old Testament that are accepted by some branches of Christianity but not by the Protestants.

The Apocrypha The term "Apocrypha" refers to a collection of Jewish writings written between 300 BC and AD 70. There are fourteen writings or portions of writings in the Apocrypha: Tobit, Judith, Additions to the Book of Esther, Wisdom of Solomon, Sirach (a.k.a. Ecclesiastes), Baruch, Epistle of Jeremiah, Song of the Three Jews, Susanna, Bel and the Dragon, 1 and 2 Maccabees, 1 Esdras, the Prayer of Manasseh, and 2 Esdras.

Of the fourteen, the Roman Catholic Counsel of Trent claimed eleven to be canonical: Tobit, Judith, Additions to the Book of Esther (added to Esther), Wisdom of Solomon, Sirach (a.k.a. Ecclesiastes), Baruch, Song of the Three Jews, Susanna, Bel and the Dragon (added to Daniel), 1 and 2 Maccabees (appearing as separate books). The Roman Catholics generally refer to them as "deuterocanonical." Geisler observes that the Council of Trent accepted 2 Maccabees, a book supporting praying for the dead (2 Maccabees 12:45 [46]), some 29 years after Luther lashed out against praying for the dead (Geisler, p. 365).

There are reasons for the rejection of the Apocrypha. For example, the New Testament copiously quotes the Old Testament but does not quote the Apocrypha. Geisler points out, "Jesus himself cited Genesis (Matt. 19:4-5), Exodus (John 6:31), Leviticus (Matt. 8:4), Numbers (John 3:14), Deuteronomy (Matt. 4:4), and I Samuel (Matt. 12:3-4). He also referred to Kings (Luke 4:25) and II Chronicles (Matt. 23:35), as well as Ezra-Nehemiah (John 6:31). Psalms is frequently quoted by Jesus (see Matt. 21:42; 22:44), Proverbs is quoted by Jesus in Luke 14:8-10 (see Provo 25:6-7), and Song of Solomon may be alluded to in John 4:10. Isaiah is often quoted by Christ (see Luke 4:18-19). Likewise, Jesus alludes to Jeremiah's Book of Lamentations (Matt. 27:30) and perhaps to Ezekiel (John 3:10). Jesus specifically quoted Daniel by name (Matt. 24:21). He also quoted passages from the twelve (minor) prophets (Matt. 26:31). Other books, such as Joshua (Heb. 13:5), Ruth (Heb. 11:32), and Jeremiah (Heb. 8:8-12), are quoted by New Testament writers. The teachings of Ecclesiastes are clearly reflected in the New Testament (*cf.* Gal. 6:7 and Eccles. 11:1 or Heb. 9:27 and Eccles. 3:2)" (Geisler, p. 356). Geisler also observes, "There is no explicit citation of

Judges, Chronicles, Esther, or the Song of Solomon, although Hebrews 11:32 refers to events in Judges, II Chronicles 24:20 may be alluded to in Matthew 23:35, Song of Solomon 4:15 may be reflected in John 4:15, and the feast of Purim established in Esther was accepted by the New Testament Jews" (Geisler, pp. 355-356).

The point is that the New Testament contains abundant references to the Old Testament but does not quote the Apocrypha. Some claim that the prophecy of Enoch in Jude 14-15 is from the apocryphal Book of Enoch. In the first place, Jude does not say he is quoting the Book of Enoch. Indeed, he may not have been. This prophecy of Enoch was no doubt handed down in Jewish tradition. For that matter, he could have gotten it from the Lord Himself. After all, Jesus was his half-brother. Furthermore, if Jude quotes the book of Enoch, it does not mean he thought the book of Enoch was inspired. Authors of inspired Scripture quote non-inspired material. It does mean, however, that it is the truth.

There are other reasons for rejecting the Apocrypha. Not only was it never quoted by Jesus or any of the New Testament writers, but it was also never recognized as Scripture by the early Christians. From the beginning, the word "Apocrypha" was used in writings not to be read in public worship but in private, generally by the more mature believers (see McDonald, p. 142). The Roman Catholic Church did not recognize the Apocrypha as Scripture until the Council of Trent in 1546.

Ryrie says, "There are some 250 quotes from Old Testament books in the New Testament. None is from the Apocrypha. All Old Testament books are quoted except Esther, Ecclesiastes, and the Song of Solomon" (Ryrie, p. 107). He also points out that in Luke 11:51, Jesus marks the extent of the Old Testament when He mentions the murders of Abel and Zechariah, but since there were other murders of God's messengers recorded in the Apocrypha after that, the Lord must not have included them in the canon (Ryrie, pp. 107-108).

Harrison says, "There was no controversy at all in connection with the books of the Apocrypha, for everyone agreed that they were non-canonical. The reason appears to have been that the works themselves simply gave no evidence whatever of having been divinely inspired. As Green and others have pointed out, some of these writings contain egregious historical, chronological, and geographical errors, quite apart from justifying falsehood and deception and making salvation dependent upon deeds of merit" (R. K. Harrison, p. 286).

Baker says, "These books were written during the gap between the testaments and while they are valuable for historical reasons, they were never considered canonical by the Jews; they are never quoted in the New Testament; they make no claim to inspiration; they contain historical inaccuracies and they are on a much lower moral and spiritual level than the canonical books" (Baker, p. 85).

Biblical Books "Certain Jewish teachers of the second century AD questioned the canonicity of Song of Solomon, Ecclesiastes, Esther, Ezekiel, and Proverbs, either because they were thought to contain contradictory statements to other parts of Scripture or did not mention the name of God, etc." (Baker, p. 85), but there is evidence from the New Testament that the Old Testament was closed in the first century, and all those books are in the Old Testament.

Conclusion: The biblical data indicate that when God spoke and men wrote, people immediately noted that what was written was the Word of God. The confirmation of the accuracy of the collections of books in the Hebrew Bible, the Protestant Old

Testament, is found in what Jesus said in Luke 24:44. The apocryphal books are not part of the collection of inspired books because they were neither sanctioned by Jesus nor by the writers of the New Testament.

The Formation of the New Testament

As with the Old Testament, based on what the Bible says, it is possible to construct a plausible scenario of how the New Testament was formed.

Biblical Data

1. God spoke. Jesus promised the apostles that the Holy Spirit would speak to them, revealing things to come. He said, "When He, the Spirit of truth, has come, He will guide you into all truth; for He will not speak on His own authority, but whatever He hears, He will speak; and He will tell you things to come" (Jn. 16:13; "holy men of God spoke as they were moved by the Holy Spirit" in 2 Pet. 1:21). This promise was given to the apostles; the Holy Spirit would guide them in all truth and declare to them things to come.

Paul claimed that he received the gospel by revelation (Gal. 1:11-12; 1 Cor. 15:3-4), that the Word of the Lord was his source for information about the rapture (1 Thess. 4:15), that Christ spoke through him (2 Cor. 13:3; 1 Cor. 7:10, 7:40; Eph. 3:3; 1 Thess. 4:1) and that he spoke in words that the Holy Spirit teaches (1 Cor. 2:13).

2. Men wrote. For example, Paul says, "If anyone thinks himself to be a prophet or spiritual, let him acknowledge that the things which I write to you are the commandments of the Lord" (1 Cor. 14:37; 2 Thess. 2:15; 2 Thess. 3:14). John says, "For I testify to everyone who hears the words of the prophecy of this book: If

anyone adds to these things, God will add to him the plagues that are written in this book; and if anyone takes away from the words of the book of this prophecy, God shall take away his part from the Book of Life, from the holy city, and from the things which are written in this book" (Rev. 22:18-19; see Jn. 21:24). McDonald says, "Clearly the author of these words believed that he had the voice of prophecy and was inspired when he wrote" (McDonald, p. 417).

3. People took note. The Jews read the Scripture in the Synagogue (Lk. 4:16-21). Believers read the Scripture in church meetings (1 Tim. 4:13). Reading a text in these meetings "implied recognition of its sacredness and authority" (McDonald, p. 144). The New Testament authors commanded that their writings should be read in public. Paul says, "I charge you by the Lord that this epistle be read to all the holy brethren" (1 Thess. 5:27; Col. 4:16). John says, "Blessed is he who reads and those who hear the words of this prophecy, and keep those things which are written in it; for the time is near" (Rev. 1:3; 2:7, 2:11, 2:17, 2:29; 3:6, 3:13, 3:22).

Discernment One of the spiritual gifts is the "discerning of spirits" (1 Cor. 12:10). John exhorted all believers: "Beloved, do not believe every spirit, but test the spirits, whether they are of God; because many false prophets have gone out into the world" (1 Jn. 4:1). Thus, by the Spirit of God, people took note that what was written was the Word of God. This is illustrated by what Paul told the Thessalonians about his preaching to them: "When you received the word of God which you heard from us, you welcomed it not as the word of men, but as it is in truth, the word of God, which also effectively works in you who believe" (1 Thess. 2:13).

Recognition There was immediate recognition that what was written was Scripture. Paul called Luke's Gospel Scripture. First

Timothy 5:18 says, "For the Scripture says, 'You shall not muzzle an ox while it treads out the grain,' and, 'The laborer is worthy of his wages.'" In this verse, Paul quotes "Scripture" and gives one reference from the Old Testament and another, which is only found in the Gospel of Luke.

Peter called Paul's writings Scripture. Peter says, "That the longsuffering of our Lord is salvation—as also our beloved brother Paul, according to the wisdom given to him, has written to you, as also in all his epistles, speaking in them of these things, in which are some things hard to understand, which those who are untaught and unstable twist to their own destruction, as they do also the rest of the Scriptures" (2 Pet. 3:15, 16). Peter speaks of "all" of Paul's epistles (2 Pet. 3:15), which indicates that Paul's epistles had already been collected. Bruce says, "Here Paul's letters seem to form a recognizable collection and to be given the status of scripture since they are associated with 'the other scriptures'" (Bruce, CS, p. 120).

Peter wrote in AD 64. Thiessen says, "The process of collecting began almost immediately after the books had been written. Peter already speaks of the Pauline epistles 'as well known'" (Thiessen, p. 7). Ryrie contends that the term 'Scripture' was 'a designation in Judaism for canonical books, so when it is used in the New Testament of other New Testament writings, it designates those writings as canonical'" (Ryrie, p. 108; see also Baker, p. 77).

The use of 2 Peter as first-century evidence for recognizing Paul's epistles as Scripture is dependent on the first-century dating of 2 Peter, which has been rejected by some who say Peter did not write 2 Peter. They reject 2 Peter as genuine because of the differences between the style and vocabulary of 1 and 2 Peter and because there is no early tradition for 2 Peter.

The epistle itself, however, bears abundant testimony to Peter's authorship. It claims to have been written by "Simon Peter" (2 Pet. 1:1). It even claims to be his second letter (2 Pet. 3:1). The author refers to the Lord's prediction about Peter's death (Jn. 21:18-19 and 2 Peter 1:14). He also claims he was an eyewitness of the transfiguration (2 Pet. 1:16-18). As Lumby says, "It is almost inconceivable that a forger, writing to warn against false teachers, writing in the interest of truth, should have thus deliberately assumed a name and experience to which he had no claim" (Thiessen, p. 288).

Concerning the differences between 1 Peter and 2 Peter, "Bigg counts 361 words in I Peter, not in II Peter, while II Peter has 231, not in I Peter. This is indeed a remarkable situation. But the truly remarkable fact is, as Ebright points out, that both epistles have a vocabulary differing much from the rest of the New Testament. 'There are seven times as many rare words in I Peter as in the New Testament taken as a whole and ten times as many in II Peter ... The noticeable difference, therefore, is not between the two Petrine epistles, but between these epistles and the rest of the New Testament'" (Biggs, cited by Hiebert, pp. 152-153). As for early evidence, Jude virtually recognized 2 Peter 2 (Jude 5-19). Zahn thinks we have an early attestation of it in the Epistle of Jude and that we really need no other" (Thiessen, p. 287).

Bruce says, "What is important is this: from the early second century onward, Paul's letters circulated not singly, but as a collection." He goes on to say, "The codex into which the letters were copied by their first editor constituted a master copy on which the letters were based" (Bruce, CS, p. 130).

To the church in Philadelphia, Jesus said, "I know your works. See, I have set before you an open door, and no one can shut it; for you have a little strength, have kept My word, and have not denied My name. Indeed, I will make those of the synagogue of Satan, who say they are Jews and are not, but lie; indeed, I will make them come and worship before your feet, and to know that I have loved you. Because you have kept My command to persevere, I also will keep you from the hour of trial which shall come upon the whole world, to test those who dwell on the earth" (Rev 3:8-10). In AD 95, Jesus, through John, could say that they had His word (Rev. 3:8) and they had kept His command (Rev. 3:10). Since they did not hear Him speak, this, at the very least, implies that they had His Word in written form. Did they not have the Gospels by this time?

Nicole suggests that a "notable parallel" exists between the establishment of the Old Testament and New Testament canons. God entrusted the Old Testament Scriptures to the Jews (Rom. 3:2), and "They were providentially guided in the recognition and preservation of the OT. Jesus and the apostles confirmed the rightness of their approach while castigating their attachment to a tradition that was superimposed on the Word of God (Matt 15:1-20; Mark 7:1-23)." Nicole says God entrusted the New Testament to His people in the churches (Nicole, p. 205).

To sum up, when God spoke and men wrote the books of the New Testament, people immediately recognized that what was written was the Word of God, and there are indications that those books were collected. God saw to it that they were recognized as His Word, preserved, and used as His Word.

The process of collecting began immediately after the New Testament books were written. Harrison points out that Colossians 4:16 refers to the "circulating of an epistle to at least one other church, and the admonition to obtain a second epistle from the other church (Laodicea) that it might be read in the church at Colosse. It is a reasonable inference that neither the writer nor the readers looked upon such documents as having only momentary value. A need for them might well arise elsewhere, warranting their preservation" (Everett Harrison, p. 92). It is hard to imagine that the believers in the church at Colosse did not copy the letter from Paul before they sent it (or a copy of it) to Laodicea.

C. F. D. Moule suggested that Luke was one of the first to collect Paul's letters. It would have been in keeping with his historian's temperament (Moule, cited by CS, p. 129). Thiessen's theory is the publication of Acts (AD 61) may have "aroused a general interest in all that Paul had written and promoted the collecting and publishing of his writings." He suggests, "Ephesus became a great Christian center during the last half of the first century, and it may well be that these Epistles were first published as a body of Pauline literature in this city." He adds, "The Synoptic Gospels were undoubtedly collected about the same time or only a little later, perhaps also at Ephesus, where the Gospel of John was published and added to the collection late in the first century. It is interesting to note that the Book of Revelation begins with a group of seven letters addressed to seven churches in Asia" (Thiessen, p. 8). Thiessen's theory is interesting because Ephesians, 1 Timothy, 1 John, and Revelation were sent to Ephesus. Warfield asserts that the canon of the New Testament was completed when John finished the book of Revelation (Warfield, p. 455).

It is reasonable to believe that by the end of the first century, there was a collection of Paul's epistles (2 Pet. 3:15) and the four Gospels, if not other New Testament books as well. McDonald, who does not think the canon was closed by the end of the first century, concedes that by the end of the first century, collections of Paul's writings "circulated freely among many churches" (McDonald, p. 321).

As with the Law of Moses, God wanted His Word used. Hence, it was to be read in the assembly. McDonald makes an interesting observation. He points out that the standard book was written on scrolls in the ancient world. This practice continued until the fourth century, when the codex began to overtake the scroll. However, it was not much later than AD 100 that the Christian community began to prefer the codex, the ancient predecessor of the modern book, over the scroll. McDonald says the codex was developed by the Romans and used for non-literary texts such as business documents, personal notes, memos, and billings. Paul often wrote letters to churches in books (codices) made of papyrus sheets or parchment. McDonald quotes Gamble, who says it was unusual for the early Christians to use the codex for their collection of Scriptures, "since it was not recognized in antiquity as a proper book. It was regarded as a mere notebook, and its associations were strictly private and utilitarian." McDonald cites the Roman poet Martial (ca. AD 80), who advised his readers to make use of the codex if they wanted to carry his poems on their journeys: "Those that parchment confines in small pages" (Epigram 1.2, LCL). Martial indicated that even the great poets' works, including Homer, Virgil, Cicero, Livy, and Ovid, were transported in this fashion. Gamble also notes that the codex could hold the contents of several scrolls. It provided the convenience of easy access and rapid referencing of material in teaching or debates with opponents.

McDonald concludes, "Because Paul made use of the codex, no doubt for convenience and portability, and because his writings were among the earliest to be acknowledged as Scripture in many churches (2 Pet 3:15-16), it is likely that he is the originator of the use of the codex in early Christianity. When his letters were collected at the end of the first century, it is likely that the use of the codex made it possible to circulate his writings in one volume" (McDonald, pp. 211-212).

Recognition in the Early Church
There is no historical record of the final formation of the New Testament. Chafer says, "No record exists as to what church first acquired a complete Bible, or the precise date of such an occurrence" (Chafer, vol. 1, p. 92). The writings, however, that have survived from the earliest times of church history indicate that the books of the New Testament were known, and there is evidence that some were recognized as Scripture.

In fact, the writings that were produced immediately after the close of the New Testament, that is, from AD 95 to AD 110, quote or allude to every book of the New Testament, assuming that 2 and 3 John are included with 1 John, which according to Goodspeed early writers, such as Irenaeus, did (see Thiessen, p. 22). See the chart on early references to the New Testament in the appendix.

Christian authors who wrote before AD 150 are sometimes called the Apostolic Fathers because of their proximity to the Apostles. Cairns lists people and writings from this period: Clement of Rome, The Epistle to Diognetus, Papias, Polycarp, Ignatius, The Didache, and the Epistle of Barnabas (Cairns, p. 72). Sometimes, The Shepherd of Hermas and Second Clement are added to that list. The definite dating of the Apostolic Fathers is debated and, in some cases, ultimately uncertain. The chronological arrangement given here is based on the content of the writing itself. First Clement is usually considered the first book to have been written after the New Testament. However, the internal evidence within the Epistle to Diognetus and the Didache suggests that they were written before the generally accepted date of First Clement. Also, there is evidence that Papias wrote earlier than is usually thought. The dates of the other works are the ones usually given.

The Epistle to Diognetus (ca. AD 100) This is an anonymous letter written by a disciple of the Apostles. The Epistle has been dated 117 (Westcott), between 120 and 130 (Ewalt), 130 (Roberts-Donaldson), 135 (Otto; Bunsen), about 150 (Lightfoot), and even later in the third century (Zahn; Harnack). The evidence from the Epistle itself suggests an early date, before 100 and possibly before 70. It speaks of Christianity as new (1:1; 2:1). Since the author says he was a disciple of the apostles (11:1; note the plural), he must have written during or shortly after their lifetime. He also speaks of the Jews making sacrifices with blood, fat, and whole burnt offerings (3:5). When the Temple was destroyed in 70, the sacrifices ceased, so this could indicate that the Epistle to Diognetus was written before 70. If so, this is the earliest non-canonical Christian writing in existence.

The author writes, "For the scriptures state clearly how God from the beginning planted a tree of life in the midst of paradise" (12:3), a reference to the book of Genesis. He quotes 1 Corinthians 8:1, stating, "the apostle says" (12:5). Many words and phrases in the book are reminiscent of the New Testament. The author refers to "the observance of months and of days" (4:5; *cf.* Gal. 4:10). He calls believers "sojourners" (5:5; *cf.* 1 Pet. 1:1). He says, "their citizenship is in heaven" (5:9; *cf.* Phil. 3:20). When they are reviled, they bless (5:5; *cf.* 1 Pet. 2:23, 39; Mt. 5:11). They are in the world, but not of the world (6:3; *cf.* Jn. 17:13-14). The One who was sent was "gentle and meek" (7:4; *cf.* 2 Cor. 10:1). He was sent as loving, not as judging (7:5; *cf.* Jn. 3:16-17). The Son died "the just for the unjust" (9:2; *cf.* 1 Pet. 3:18). God sent "His only begotten Son" (10:2; Jn. 3:16). God promised the kingdom and will give it to those who love Him (10:2; *cf.* Jas. 2:5). He says, "You love Him that so loved you before" (10:2; *cf.* 1 Jn. 4:19). Believers are "imitators of God" (10:6; Eph. 5:1) "He sent forth the Word, that He might appear unto the world, who being dishonored by the people, and preached by the Apostles, was believed in by the Gentiles" (11:3; *cf.* 1 Tim. 3:16). The Word was from the beginning (11:4; *cf.* Jn. 1:1). "The apostles say, "Knowledge puffs up, but charity edifies" (12:5; *cf.* 1 Cor. 8:1). In other words, the author knew 1 Corinthians and, no doubt, nine other New Testament books (Jn.; 2 Cor.; Gal.; Eph.; Phil.; 1 Tim.; Titus; Jas.; and 1 Pet.).

Thiessen says the letter contains language resembling 2 Cor. 6:8-10 (ch. v, Thiessen, p. 207), speaks of "observing months and days" as in Galatians 4:10 (ch. iv, Thiessen, p. 213), seems to allude to Philippians 3:20 (ch. v, Thiessen, p. 247), has a possible reminiscence of Titus 3:4 (ch. ix) and of 1 Tim. 3:16 (ch. xi, Thiessen, p. 254) and seems to allude to the idea in 1 John 4:19 (ch. 10, Thiessen, p. 306; Everett Harrison, p. 411).

Didache The Didache is also known as the Teaching of the Twelve Apostles. Although some date the work in the middle of the second century (Harnack dates it after 131; Cairns, in the middle of the second century, p. 77), many have argued for a date before 100. It speaks of apostles and prophets coming to minister (Didache 11:5-9). There is no mention in early literature of apostles later than in the apostolic age. Clement and Ignatius do not even mention itinerant ministers. Moreover, the Didache speaks of the twofold ministries of bishops and deacons (Didache 15:1-2). Some say it was written between 80 and 90 (Bartlet), and others say before 70 (Sabatier; Minasi; Jacquier). Ehrman says it appears to have been written "at the same time as or possibly even earlier than some of the books of the New Testament" (Ehrman, vol. 1, p. 165). Jonathan Zdziarski, a scientist who has studied and translated the Didache, dates it between AD 49 and 79 (see www.zdziarski.com/papers/didache). The dating of the Didache at 49 is probably too early; however, dating it before 100, or even between 80 and 90, is reasonable. (McDonald says it was likely written between AD 70 and 120.)

There are quotations and numerous allusions to the Gospel of Matthew. For example, the author says, "Neither pray like the hypocrites, but as the Lord has commanded in His Gospel, in this way pray" (Didache 8:2). The author quotes the entire Lord's Prayer, including the ending omitted by the modern Critical Text (Didache 8:2-7). He also states, "The meek will inherit the land" (Didache 3:7). Several times, he mentions being double-minded (Didache 2:4; 4:4), reminiscent of James 1:8. There are allusions to other books of the New Testament, including slaves being told to be subject to their masters Didache 4:11; cf. Eph. 6:5; Col. 3:22), believers being told not to eat meat sacrificed to idols (Didache 6:3; cf. Acts 15:29), believers being instructed that if people do not work, do not let them live with you idle (Didache 12:4; 2 Thess. 3:11-12), and prophets are worthy of their food as workmen are worthy of theirs (Didache 13:1-2; 1 Tim. 5:17).

The author admonishes his readers: "And reprove one another not in wrath but in peace as you find in the Gospel, and let none speak with any who has done wrong to his neighbor, nor let him hear a word from you until he repents. But your prayers, alms, and all your acts perform as ye find in the Gospel of our Lord" (Didache 15.3-4). Harrison says, "Numerous citations from Matthew are used, but without naming the source" (Everett Harrison, p. 94). Thiessen says, "It uses Matthew a good deal and Luke some," and "it knows most of our New Testament books" (Thiessen, p. 13).

Clement of Rome Clement of Rome wrote to the church at Corinth. His letter was written early. It refers to the deaths of Peter and Paul as 'belong[ing] to our generation" (Clement 5:1-5). On the other hand, it is not too early because it refers to the Corinthian church as "ancient" (Clement 47:7) and speaks of some members who had been Christians "from youth to old age" (Clement, 63:3). It should also be noted that 1 Clement was written soon after a period of persecution (Clement 1:1). If that was the persecution of Nero, the epistle was written about 68. If the persecution referred to was that of Domitian, the epistle was written at the close of the first century or the beginning of the second. A date of about 97 is the one generally accepted.

First Clement contains abundant references to the writings of the New Testament. In one instance, Clement says, "Most of all, remembering the words of our Lord Jesus Christ, which He spoke, teaching forbearance and longsuffering; for this, He spoke." He then quotes from Christ's Sermon on the Mount (chapter 13; *cf.* Mt. 5:7; 6:14, 15; 7:1, 12, 14; Lk. 16:31, 36-38). Some have argued that he is quoting from oral tradition rather than the written Gospels, but in chapter 46, he again says, "Remember the words of our Lord Jesus for He said," and this time records a saying of Christ recorded in Matthew 18:6; 26:24; Mark 9:42; 14:21, and Luke 17:1, 2. Clement may be quoting Matthew, Mark, Luke, or all three. Lightfoot affirms that Clement used written Gospels (Everett Harrison, p. 93). He uses phraseology from the New Testament, such as telling the Corinthians that they were "more glad to give than to receive" (Acts 20:35) and "ready unto every good work" (chapter 2; *cf.* Titus 3:1) and he calls the apostles like Peter and Paul "pillars" (Gal. 2:9) of the church (chapter 5).

In 1 Clement chapter 2, there is a possible allusion to Galatians 3:1 (*cf.* "an abundant outpouring of the Holy Spirit fell upon all") and in chapter 45 to 2 Timothy 1:3 (*cf.* "pure conscience"). At least twice, he seems to be alluding to the book of Romans. He says, "Of Him (that is, God) is the Lord Jesus, as according to the flesh" (chapter 32; *cf.* Rom. 9:5) and "for they that do these things are hateful to God and not only that do them, but they also that consent to do them" (chapter 35; *cf.* Rom. 1:32).

Clement refers to Ephesians 4:4-6 in chapter 46, saying, "Have we not one God and one Christ and one Spirit of grace that was shed upon us? Is there not one calling in Christ?" Who could doubt that Clement had James 3:1 in mind when he says, "Let the wise display his wisdom not in words, but in good works" (chapter 38)? The same could be said of his use of James 3:16.

Clement borrows from Hebrews on several occasions. Speaking of the Lord Jesus, he says, "Being the brightness of his Majesty is so much greater than angels as He inherited a more excellent name. For so it is written, 'Who made His angels spirits and His ministers a flame of fire,' but of His Son, the Master said thus, 'Thou art My Son; I this day have begotten Thee. Ask of me and I will give Thee the Gentiles for Thine inheritance, and the ends of the earth for Thy Possession.' And again, He said unto Him, 'Sit Thou on My right hand until I make Thine enemies a footstool for Thy feet'" (*cf.* 1 Clement 36 with Heb. 1:2, 3, 4, 6,

13). He says Moses was "a faithful servant in all his house" (*cf.* 1 Clement 43 with Heb. 3:5). In chapter 17, he said, "Let us become imitators also of those who went about in goatskins and sheepskins" (Heb. 11:37).

In chapter 7, there is an allusion to 1 Peter, where Clement says, "Let us fix our eyes on the blood of Christ and understand how precious it is to His Father" (1 Pet. 1:19). In chapter 34, he says, "Since he forewarned us, saying, 'Behold the Lord and His reward is before His face to recompense each man according to his work" (Rev. 22:12).

While some of these references in 1 Clement are mere allusions to the New Testament, there can be absolutely no doubt that he knew about 1 Corinthians. In chapter 47, he said, "Take up the epistle of the blessed Paul the apostle. What wrote he first unto you in the beginning of the gospel? Of a truth, he charged you in the Spirit concerning himself and Cephas and Apollos because that even then ye had made parties." Is there not a reference to 2 Corinthians 13:8 in Clement's statement, "Through Him let us look steadfastly into the heights of the heavens. Through Him, we behold as in a mirror His faultless and most excellent visage?" (chapter 36).

There is no question that Clement was familiar with the writings of the New Testament. He either quotes or alludes to Matthew, Mark, Luke, Acts, Romans, 1 and 2 Corinthians, Galatians, Ephesians, 2 Timothy, Titus, Hebrews, James, 1 Peter, and the book of Revelation. Moreover, Clement wrote, "Take up the epistle of the blessed Apostle Paul. What did he write to you at the time when the Gospel first began to be preached? Truly, under the inspiration of the Spirit, he wrote to you concerning himself, and Cephas, and Apollos, because even then parties had been formed among you" (1 Clement 47:1-3). Clement of Rome said Paul wrote to the Corinthians "under the inspiration of the Spirit!"

Papias One of the leaders in the church of Hierapolis in Phrygia, about 100 miles east of Ephesus, was Papias. According to Irenaeus, he was "the hearer of John and a companion of Polycarp" (Irenaeus, Ag. Her. 5.33.4). Scholars disagree concerning the date for Papias. In an article entitled "The Date of Papias: A Reassessment," Robert W. Yarborough lists the reasons for a late date and gives the evidence for an early date (Yarborough, JETS, volume 26, pp. 181-182). Yarborough argues that Papias is likely to have written between *ca.* 95 and 110.

Papias was the author of five books entitled the *Interpretations of the Sayings of the Lord*, which unfortunately have disappeared, except for a few fragments that are recorded in the writings of Irenaeus (Papias, Against Heresies, 5:33.4, 5:36.1-2) and Eusebius (Eusebius, Eccl. Hist., 3:39.3-5, 15-16; see 3:24 for Eusebius' view). The Eusebius section says Matthew wrote his work in Hebrew, and Mark was Peter's interpreter (Cairns, p. 76). Papias mentions Matthew and Mark, quotes 1 John and 1 Peter, and knows John's gospel (Thiessen, p. 13).

According to Yarborough, the implications of the early date are 1) another voice, perhaps the earliest, to the early authorship and circulation of 1 John and 1 Peter (Eusebius, Eccl. Hist., 3.39. 17); 2) verification of the tradition of the aged apostle John's ministry in Asia Minor (Eusebius, Eccl. Hist., 3.39.3-4); 3) an indication that Mark's Gospel comprises Peter's preaching (Eusebius, Eccl. Hist., 3.39.15); and 4) an indication that Matthew wrote a gospel in Hebrew (G. Kittel, "Logion," TDNT vol. 4, pp. 140-141). To that list could be added that most agree Papias refers to the story of the woman taken in adultery (Morris in his commentary on the

Gospel of John, p. 883; he cites Eusebius, Eccl. Hist., 3:39, 17).

Polycarp (AD 69-155) Polycarp was Bishop of Smyrna. He wrote a letter to the Philippians around AD 110 (Cairns, p. 75) and was burned at the stake in AD 155 at the age of 86 (Cairns, pp. 74-75). According to his pupil, Irenaeus, Polycarp was a student of John the Apostle. Polycarp's epistle (ca. AD 110) contains about sixty quotations from the New Testament, thirty-four of which are from the writings of Paul (Cairns, p. 75). He refers to Paul being at Philippi and writing them a letter (chapter 2). To be more specific, he quotes 14 books of the New Testament, including Matthew, Luke, Acts, Romans, 1 Corinthians, Galatians, Ephesians, Philippians, 1 Timothy, 2 Timothy, 1 Thessalonians, 2 Thessalonians, 1 Peter, and 1 John (Thiel claims that Polycarp alludes to all 27 books of the NT; for his proof see www.COGwriter.com).

Harrison says his letter to the Philippians, which he dates ca. 115, "abounds with language drawn from the New Testament. More than once, statements are attributed to Jesus, introduced by the words, 'The Lord said.' In citing Paul, Polycarp several times uses the introductory phrase, 'knowing that,' which Lightfoot takes to be a formula of citation (see 1:15; 5:1). Most striking is the quoting of Psalm 4:5, 'Be angry and sin not,' followed immediately by Ephesians 4:26, 'Let not the sun go down upon your wrath,' and the prefacing of the combined statements with the words, 'as it is said in these Scriptures' (12: 1)" (Everett Harrison, p. 94). McDonald says, "Polycarp appears to have consciously placed an OT Scripture and a Christian writing on an equal authoritative footing" (McDonald, p. 276). Kistemaker concurs, saying, "Polycarp considers Paul's letter to the Ephesians Scripture and to be equal to the OT" (Kistemaker, p. 8).

It is Reasonable To Believe God's Message Is Accurate: Part 1

In his book *Early Christian Doctrines*, J. N. D. Kelly, an Oxford professor, contends that Polycarp's citations of Paul's epistles indicate that a collection of them existed at Smyrna (Kelly, p. 58). He adds that the numerous apparent echoes of Paul's epistles in Clement perhaps indicate that he was acquainted with a nucleus of Paul's epistles as early as 95 (Kelly, p. 58).

Ehrman states that part of the reason Polycarp wrote to the Philippians was their request for the collection of Ignatius' letters (Ehrman, vol. 1, p. 100). Here is what Polycarp said: "Ye wrote to me, both ye yourselves and Ignatius, asking that if anyone should go to Syria, he might carry thither the letters from you. And I will do this if I get a fit opportunity, either myself or he whom I shall send to be an ambassador on your behalf. The letters of Ignatius, which were sent to us by him, and others as many as we had by us, we send unto you, according as ye gave charge; the which are subjoined to this letter; from which ye will be able to gain great advantage. For they comprise faith and endurance and every kind of edification, which pertains unto our Lord" (Polycarp, Philippians 13).

Pointing out that Polycarp was from Smyrna, Ehrman explains that Ignatius wrote four of his seven letters from Smyrna (Ephesians, Magnesians, Trallians, and Romans), sent two of the letters to Smyrna (Smyrna and the letter to Polycarp), and sent the seventh letter to Philadelphia, which was not far from Smyrna. Ehrman states that copies of these letters were evidently kept in the church at Smyrna, and he even suggests that the collection of Ignatius' letters was originally compiled by Polycarp himself (Ehrman, vol. 1, p. 101).

If Christians collected the writings of Ignatius, surely they collected the writings of the Apostles, those associated with them

(Mark, Luke, Barnabas, who probably wrote Hebrews), and the half-brothers of Jesus (James and Jude). Granted, this does not prove the exact 27 books of the New Testament were collected, but it does demonstrate that Christians collected spiritual writings early in the second century (110).

Ignatius Ignatius was from Antioch in Syria and wrote seven letters about AD 110 (Cairns, p. 74; McDonald dates him ca. AD 100-107, p. 275). There are two versions of his writings; one is shorter than the other. Ignatius quotes Matthew 13:33 (Eph. 14), 1 Cor. 6:9-10 (Eph. 16), 2 Cor. 4:18 (Rom. 3), and 1 Thess. 5:17 (Polycarp 1). In Ephesians 5, he quotes, "God resists the proud" (Prov. 3:34; Jas. 4:6; 1 Pet. 5:5). He alludes to Matthew 18:19 (Eph. 5), 1 Pet. 2:5 (Eph. 9), and John 12:7 (Eph. 17). Writing to the Ephesians, Ignatius uses phrases from the New Testament book of Ephesians (cf. his Eph. 1 with Eph. 5:2). In addition, in the longer version, he quotes Colossians 2:10 and 1 Timothy 4:10 (Eph. 8); John 14:6, (Eph. 9); 2 Tim. 2:24-25 (Eph. 10); 1 Pet. 2:23 (Eph. 10); Luke 23:34 (Eph. 10); Ephesians 6:12 (Eph. 13); Romans 10:10 (Eph. 15); 2 Cor. 6:14-16 (Eph. 14); 1 Cor. 1:18 (Eph. 18); Luke 6:46 (Magnesians 4); John 5:30 (Magnesians 7); 2 Thess. 3:10 (Magnesians 9). He also says Paul wrote to the Ephesians (Eph. 6). Ignatius knew the New Testament in general, especially the epistles of Paul, but Matthew and the Gospel of John are his favorites (Thiessen, p. 12). He "carefully distinguishes his own position from that of the apostles" (Everett Harrison, p. 94).

Quadratus Quadratus was one of the first Christian apologists. Jerome said that Quadratus represents an apology (a defense of Christianity) to Hadrian. Hadrian reigned as Emperor of Rome from 117 to 138. Eusebius quotes Quadratus as saying that some who were healed were still alive, which would probably put his date closer to 117 than 138. The only surviving writing of Quadratus is a short passage recorded by Eusebius. It does not contain any quotations from Scripture, but it does say, "The works of our Savior were always present, for they were genuine: those that were healed, and those that were raised from the dead, who were seen not only when they were healed and when they were raised but were also always present; and not merely while the Savior was on earth, but also after his death, they were alive for quite a while, so that some of them lived even to our day" (Eusebius, Hist. Eccl. 4.1-2).

To sum up, the canon per se was not discussed during this period (AD 95-110), but the writings that were produced immediately after the close of the New Testament quote or allude to every book of the New Testament. The author of The Didache (*ca.* AD 80-90) knew most of our New Testament books. Clement of Rome (AD 95) calls 1 Corinthians inspired. Papias (AD 95-110) wrote an Exposition of the Oracles of the Lord (that is, Scripture). He mentions Matthew and Mark, quotes 1 John and 1 Peter, and is familiar with John's Gospel. Polycarp (AD 110) quotes 14 books of the New Testament and considers Paul's letter to the Ephesians Scripture to be equal to the Old Testament. Ignatius (AD 110) carefully distinguished himself from the apostles, knew Matthew and John, the New Testament in general, and the epistles of Paul.

Kistemaker concludes, "Clement of Rome, Ignatius, Polycarp, and others did not hesitate to accept the letters of Paul and regard them as Scripture. Donald Hagnet notes, 'The Apostolic Fathers are essentially united in their witness to the authority of the new writings; there is no radical change in the valuation of these writings between AD 95 and AD 140'" (Kistemaker, p. 8).

It is also important to note that the men who wrote immediately after the close of the New Testament did not claim to write Scripture. Kistemaker observes, "Clement of Rome says that his own letter has been 'written through the Holy Spirit' (1 Clem. 63:2). Near the end of the second century, he is referred to as "apostle Clement" by Clement of Alexandria. And Eusebius, commenting on Clement's letter, says that it enjoyed recognition in the churches because, in earlier times, as well as his own, it was read publicly in the assemblies (*Church History* 3:15-16). First Clement, however, is not listed as Scripture in sub-apostolic times. This is rather remarkable in view of the fact that both John's Revelation and Clement's first epistle were written in AD 95. Revelation is part of the NT canon; 1 Clement is not. Irenaeus held 1 Clement in high esteem without granting it any status. Except for its inclusion in Codex Alexandrinus, a document of the fifth century, 1 Clement has never been accepted as canonical" (Kistemaker, p. 7).

Kistemaker also says, "Do the apostolic fathers place themselves on a level with the writers of the NT? The answer must be negative. Clement of Rome, Ignatius, and Polycarp do not claim divine authority for themselves. Ignatius speaks with authority when he addresses the churches in his letters. However, he does not put himself in the same category as the apostles. In his letter to the Romans, he writes: "I do not order you as did Peter and Paul; they were Apostles, I am a convict" (4:3; tr. Kirsopp Lake). Also, in his letter to the Trallians, Ignatius deprecates himself: "I am sparing you in my love, though I might write more sharply on his behalf: I did not think myself competent, as a convict, to give orders like an Apostle" (3:3; tr. Kirsopp Lake) (Kistemaker, p. 10).

It is Reasonable To Believe God's Message Is Accurate: Part 1

The Debate about the New Testament

Some books in the Bible were questioned, while others not in our Bible were regarded as Scripture. Thiessen says, "Generally speaking, from the time of Irenaeus on, the New Testament contained practically the same books as we receive today and were regarded with the same reverence that we bestow on them today." He adds that a minority continued to question the authenticity of some of the books for a long time (Thiessen, p. 10). It should not surprise the child of God that some would doubt anything connected with God. Doubt was the original tool of Satan (Gen. 3:1). Doubt, differences of opinion, and even division are not only normal; they are also necessary. Paul explains, "For first of all, when you come together as a church, I hear that there are divisions among you, and in part I believe it. For there must also be factions among you, that those who are approved may be recognized among you" (1 Cor. 11:18-19). Differences are needed to help the discerning determine the truth.

Overview In the third and fourth centuries, some of the books of the New Testament were debated. Ryrie says, "Most of the New Testament books were received; only a few were debated" (Ryrie, p. 109).

Origen (*ca.* AD 185-254, Cairns, p. 111) recognized a New Testament collection alongside the Old Testament (Bruce, CS, p. 192). He distinguished between the homologoumena, the books universally recognized as Scripture, and the antilegomena, the books more or less opposed. In the former group, he included the four Gospels, Acts, thirteen Epistles of Paul, 1 Peter, 1 John, and Revelation; in the latter, he placed Hebrews, James, 2 Peter, 2 and 3 John, Jude, Barnabas, the Shepherd, the Didache, and the Gospel of the Hebrews (Thiessen, pp. 10-11).

He placed Hebrews in the latter category because some churches did not accept it (Bruce, CS, p. 193). Origen himself, however, frequently cited Hebrews as canonical and referred to all the other New Testament books as Scripture, except for Jude, 2 John, and 3 John (Thiessen, p. 11). So, even though Origen speaks of opposing books, he accepts all the New Testament books, except Jude, 2 John, and 3 John. Thiessen states that Souter believes it is possible that Origen recognized them as genuine (Thiessen, p. 18). There is no evidence that Origen personally rejected any of the New Testament books on the list of opposition.

Bruce explains that Origen "mentions all twenty-seven books of our New Testament; twenty-one, he says, are acknowledged, and six are doubtful. But among doubtful books, he also reckons some which, in the end, did not secure a place in the canon. Like Clement of Alexandria before him, he treats the Didache as scripture and calls the Letter of Barnabas a 'catholic epistle'—a term he also applies to 1 Peter. R. M. Grant suggests that while he lived in Alexandria, he accepted the more comprehensive tradition of the church there and acknowledged the Didache and the Letter of Barnabas, together with the Shepherd of Hermas, as scripture, but that after he moved to Caesarea and found that these books were not accepted there, he manifested greater reserve towards them. He knew 1 Clement but did not indicate if he regarded it as scripture. He had doubts about the Preaching of Peter, which Clement of Alexandria regarded highly. He refers to the Gospel according to the Hebrews and the Acts of Paul without at first either admitting or disputing their status as scripture; later, however, he had doubts about the Acts of Paul" (Bruce, CS, p. 194).

Eusebius of Caesarea (ca. AD 260-ca. 340, Cairns, p. 143) was the first to attempt a comprehensive history of the church on a grand scale. He began his Ecclesiastical History in either AD 303 or AD 313. He eventually brought the story up to AD 324.

Like Origen, he distinguished between the homologoumena and the antilegomena but divided the latter into merely disputed and spurious ones. In other words, he had three categories: the recognized, the disputed, and the spurious. Under the recognized, he lists the four Gospels, Acts, the Epistles of Paul, 1 John, 1 Peter, and Revelation. Under those merely disputed, he mentions James, 2 Peter, 2 and 3 John, and Jude. Under those actually spurious, he lists the Acts of Paul, the Shepherd, the Apocalypse of Peter, Barnabas, the Didache, and perhaps Revelation. He lists Revelation under both the dispute and the spurious category!

Here is what Eusebius says: "At this point, it seems reasonable to summarize the writings of the New Testament which have been quoted. In the first place, the holy tetrad of the Gospels. To them follows the writing of the Acts of the Apostles. After this should be reckoned the Epistles of Paul. Following them, the Epistle of John is called the first, and, in the same way, should be recognized the Epistle of Peter. In addition to these should be put, if it seems desirable, the Revelation of John, the arguments concerning which we will expound at the proper time. These belong to the Recognized Books [homologoumenois]. Of the Disputed Books [ton d' antilegoumenon], which are nevertheless known to most, are the Epistle called of James, that of Jude, the Second Epistle of Peter, and the so-called second and third Epistles of John, which may be the work of the evangelist or of some other with the same name. Among the books which are not genuine [en tois nothois] must be reckoned the Acts of Paul, the work entitled the Shepherd, the Apocalypse of Peter, and, in addition to them, the letter called of Barnabas and the so-called Teachings of the Apostles [Didache].

And in addition, as I said, the Revelation of John, if this view prevails. For, as I said, some reject it, but others count it among the Recognized Books. Some have also counted the Gospel according to the Hebrews, in which those of the Hebrews who have accepted Christ take a special pleasure. These would all belong to the disputed books, but we have nevertheless been obliged to make a list of them, distinguishing between those writings which, according to the tradition of the Church [lit., ecclesiastical tradition], are true, genuine, and recognized [scriptures] [aletheis kai aplastous kai anomologemenas graphas], and those which differ from them in that they are not canonical [ouk endiathekous] but disputed, yet nevertheless are own to most of the writers of the Church, in order that we might know them and the writings which are put forward by heretics under the name of the apostles containing gospels such as those of Peter, and Thomas, and Matthias, and some others besides, or Acts such as those of Andrew and John and the other apostles. To none of these has anyone who belonged to the succession of the orthodox ever thought it right to refer in his writings. Moreover, the type of phraseology differs from apostolic style, and the opinion and tendency of their contents are widely dissonant from true orthodoxy and clearly show that they are the forgeries of heretics. They ought, therefore, to be reckoned not even among spurious [en notboisl books but shunned as altogether wicked and impious" (Eusebius, Hist. Eccl. 3.25.1-7).

Observations First, to summarize: during the third and fourth centuries, some doubted the authenticity of Hebrews, James, 2 Peter, 2 and 3 John, Jude, and Revelation. Origen reports that some doubted certain books, but he himself accepts all the books of the New Testament, except for 2 and 3 John and Jude; some scholars think it is possible that Origen recognized them as genuine. There is no evidence that Origen personally rejected any of the New Testament books on the opposed list. Eusebius lists James, 2 Peter, 2 and 3 John, and Jude as disputed, not spurious. For some reason, Eusebius fails to mention the Book of Hebrews and places Revelation in both the disputed and spurious categories. Thus, in some quarters, there were some questions about seven books: Hebrews, James, 2 Peter, 2 and 3 John, Jude, and the Revelation. These books lacked "universal endorsement" (Everett Harrison, p. 101).

Second, there were different reasons why these "doubted books" were questioned.

Hebrews was questioned because of its authorship (Everett Harrison, p. 345). There is, however, abundant evidence for it dating back to early times. For example, Clement of Rome (AD 95) quotes it copiously and cites several first-century authors (Thiessen, pp. 297-298).

James was perhaps questioned because it was written to Jewish believers and contained little that would appeal to the "speculative mind of Greek Christians" (Tenney, p. 427). The Muratorian Fragment omitted it. Eusebius classified it as disputed but quoted it as Scripture (Eusebius, *Commentary on the Psalms*). Mayor quotes early authors beginning with Clement of Rome and concludes that James "was more widely known during the first three centuries than has been commonly supposed" (Mayor, pp. lii-lxviii).

In his preface to the New Testament, Luther described James as "a perfect straw epistle," in comparison to the Gospel of John, 1 John, the epistles of Paul, especially Romans, Galatians, Ephesians, and Peter's epistles. He complained that James did not include the gospel. Luther placed Hebrews, James, Jude, and

Revelation at the end of his German New Testament, assigning them no numbers in the table of contents. Harrison says Luther distrusted James and was disappointed in it (Everett Harrison, p. 360). Ryrie observes, "Sometimes it is claimed that Martin Luther rejected the Book of James as being canonical. This is not so. Here's what he wrote in his preface to the New Testament, in which he ascribes different degrees of doctrinal value to the several books of the New Testament. 'St. John's Gospel and his first Epistle, St. Paul's Epistles, especially those to the Romans, Galatians, Ephesians, and St. Peter's Epistle—these are the books which show to thee Christ and teach everything necessary and blessed for thee to know, even if you were never to see or hear any other book of doctrine. Therefore, St. James' Epistle is a perfect straw-epistle compared with them, for it has in it nothing of an evangelic kind." Thus Luther was comparing (in his opinion) doctrinal value, not canonical validity" (Ryrie, p. 109). The Lutheran Church has not followed Luther's evaluation of James.

Second Peter was questioned because of its difference in style from 1 Peter. Jerome says some hesitation in accepting 2 Peter was because it was so different from 1 Peter (Jerome, *Epistle to Hedibia*, 120; see also Tenney, p. 427). Even Calvin was unsure of 2 Peter (Tenney, p. 428)! Lumby says, "It is almost inconceivable that a forger, writing to warn against false teachers, writing in the interest of truth, should have thus deliberately assumed a name and experience to which he had no claim" (Thiessen, p. 288). Could it be that some reject this letter because it rejects them?

Second John was questioned perhaps because there were few early quotations or definite allusions to it. Irenaeus attributes 2 John 11 to John, the disciple of the Lord (Irenaeus, Against Heresies I. xvi. 3) and assigns 2 John 7-8 to the Apostle John

(Irenaeus, Against Heresies III. xvi. 8). Origen says some doubted it, but he does not seem to reject it (Everett Harrison, p. 422).

Third John was questioned probably for the same reason as 2 John. The evidence for it is less than for 2 John, but as has been mentioned, Goodspeed claims that the early writers included 2 and 3 John with 1 John, which is what Irenaeus did (see Thiessen, p. 22).

Jude was questioned for several reasons. Eusebius lists it as a disputed book but in another place, calls it spurious because not many ancients made use of it (Eusebius, Hist. Eccl. II. xxiii. 25). Jerome says some rejected it because of its supposed reference to the book of Enoch (Jerome, Lives of Illustrious Men, ch. 4). On the other hand, Tertullian considered Enoch Scripture, because of Jude's use of it!

Thiessen explains: "Clement of Alexandria, Tertullian, Jerome, Augustine, and the Church Fathers generally held that Jude quotes from several apocryphal books. It was on this ground that they long rejected it. It was held that at verse 9, the writer quotes from the Assumption of Moses, and at verses 14-15, from the Book of Enoch. Philippi vigorously denied this, saying that Jude merely wrote from oral tradition, which is a possible explanation. The fragment of the Assumption of Moses that has come down to us is broken off before the burial of Moses is reached, and we really cannot tell what followed in the part that is missing. There is a great similarity between Enoch 1:9; 5:4 and Jude 14 f. Moorehead admits the possibility of a quotation in both instances. Concerning the Book of Enoch in particular, he says: 'Granting such a quotation, that fact does not warrant us to affirm that he endorses the book. Paul cites from three Greek poets: from Aratus (Acts 17:28), from Menander, and from Epimenides the apostle adds,

'This testimony is true' (Tit. 1:13), but no one imagines he means to say the whole poem is true' (Tit. 1:13). So Jude cites a passage from a non-canonical book not because he accepts the whole book as true, but this particular prediction he receives as from God.' This seems to us to be a satisfactory solution to the problem" (Thiessen, pp. 294-295).

Revelation was not questioned at first. Harrison points out, "John's Apocalypse had a solid place in the canon in the earlier patristic period, being questioned only by the sect known as the Alogi, but generally received throughout the church. The failure of writers in the East during the fourth century to include it in the New Testament may be assigned to the influence of the criticism of Dionysius of Alexandria, who argued the great differences between the Revelation and the Fourth Gospel as ground for concluding that another John must have written the Apocalypse. Influenced by Dionysius, Eusebius felt that it was wise to put the book not only among the acknowledged writings (Homologoumena) but also with the non-genuine, saying that some reject it" (Everett Harrison, p. 101).

Baker says, "By the end of the fourth century, the doubts associated with these seven books were removed and all were accepted as canonical" (Baker, p. 85).

The Rejected Books

It should not surprise the child of God that some would attempt to imitate the Word of God. "Satan himself transforms himself into an angel of light" (2 Cor. 11:14). Even in Paul's day, false teachers circulated letters purportedly written by him (2 Thess. 2:2).

Spurious Books In the early centuries of church history, some books were accepted as canonical that are not in the Protestant

New Testament. According to Baker, "The New Testament Apocrypha consists of gospels and epistles written under the name of an apostle or a well-known leader. Some fifteen of these extra-canonical books have been listed: The Teaching of the Twelve Apostles, The Epistle of Barnabas, The First Epistle of Clement, the Second Epistle of Clement, The Shepard of Hermas, The Apocalypse of Peter, The Acts of Paul, including Paul and Thecla, The Epistle of Polycarp to the Philippians, The Seven Epistles of Ignatius, The Gospel of Pseudo-Matthew, The Protevangelium of James, The Gospel of the Nativity of Mary, The Gospel of Nicodemus, The Gospel of the Savior's Infancy, and the History of Joseph the Carpenter" (Baker, pp. 85-86).

Harrison suggests that some books were considered canonical by some Christians because they were thought to be apostolic. He points out that the full name of the Didache is the Teaching of the Twelve Apostles. Clement of Rome was considered to be the Clement mentioned in Philippians 4:3 (Clement of Alexander, Origen). The acceptance of the Shepherd of Hermas in some quarters is traced to the belief that the author was the one mentioned in Romans 16:14 (Everett Harrison, pp. 104-105).

Eusebius explains, "Some have also counted [as canonical or recognized] the Gospel according to the Hebrews, in which those of the Hebrews who have accepted Christ take a special pleasure. These would all belong to the disputed books, but we have nevertheless been obliged to make a list of them, distinguishing between those writings which, according to the tradition of the Church, are true, genuine, and recognized and those which differ from them in that they are not canonical but disputed, yet nevertheless are known to most of the writers of the Church, in order that we might know them and the writings which are put forward by heretics under the name of the apostles containing gospels such as those of Peter, and Thomas, and Matthias, and some others besides, or Acts such as those of Andrew and John and the other apostles. To none of these has anyone who belonged to the succession of the orthodox ever thought it right to refer in his writings. Moreover, the type and phraseology differ from apostolic style, and the opinion and tendency of their contents are widely dissonant from true orthodoxy, clearly showing that they are the forgeries of heretics. They ought, therefore, to be reckoned not even among spurious books but shunned as altogether wicked and impious" (Eusebius, Hist. Eccl. 3.25:6-7).

The Shepherd of Hermas (ca. AD 150) Irenaeus regarded The Shepherd of Hermas as Scripture. Clement of Alexandria said that it made its statements "divinely" and although Origen seems to express doubts about it, he recognized it as divinely inspired. Sinaiticus (fourth century) lists Hermas with the canonical books of the New Testament (Kistemaker, p. 7).

The Muratorian Fragment (AD 170) says, "The Shepherd was written by Hermas in the city of Rome quite recently, in our own times, when his brother Pius occupied the bishop's chair in the church of the city of Rome; and therefore it may be read indeed, but cannot be given out to the people in church either among the prophets, since their number is complete, or among the apostles at the end of the times" (cited by Bruce, CS, p. 161).

Before Tertullian (AD 160-225) became a Montanist, he included the Shepherd of Hermas in his collection of Scriptures, but he later dismissed it "with scorn" (McDonald, p. 304). In his treatise on modesty (chap. 10), he states that the Shepherd of Hermas had been "habitually judged by every council of churches … among apocryphal and false (writings)."

The point is that there were spurious books claiming to be from the apostles, and some Christians did accept a few of them, but the early Church was aware of this problem and rejected those books that were not inspired.

The Saying of Jesus According to the Apostle John, besides what is recorded in his gospel, "many other things that Jesus did, which if they were written one by one, I suppose that even the world itself could not contain the books that would be written" (Jn. 21:25). Surely, not all of the sayings of Jesus are recorded in the four Gospels of the New Testament.

Sure enough, there are sayings of Jesus that have been recorded outside the New Testament. In fact, there are 266 supposed sayings of Jesus not found in the canonical Gospels (called agrapha). The problem is determining if any of these are authentic and, if so, which ones. Jeremias has stated that only eighteen are authentic (McDonald, p. 8, fn. 8, 282). Even if we could determine that one or more of the sayings were genuine, evidently, God did not intend that they be part of His inspired Word; that alone is sufficient to bring believers to spiritual maturity and equip them for every good work (2 Tim. 3:16-17). In other words, even a genuine saying of Jesus recorded outside the Bible is not part of God's Word.

The Gospel of the Infancy of Jesus Christ This book contains the story of some sisters whose brother was bewitched by a woman and turned into a mule. The sisters came to the Virgin Mary for help: "Hereupon St. Mary was grieved at their case, and taking the Lord Jesus, put him upon the back of the mule. And said to her son, O Jesus Christ, restore according to thy extraordinary power this mule, and grant him to have again the shape of a man and a rational creature, as he had formerly. This was scarce said by the Lady St. Mary, but the mule immediately passed into a human form, and became a young man without any deformity" (The Gospel of the Infancy of Jesus Christ 7:24-26).

The Epistle of Barnabas In discussing the dietary laws of Leviticus, The Epistle of Barnabas says, "Neither shalt thou eat of the hyena; that is, again, be not an adulterer, nor a corruptor of others; neither be like to such. And wherefore so?-because that creature every year changes its kind, and is sometimes male and sometimes female" (The Epistle of Barnabas 9:8).

The Gospel of Thomas According to The Gospel of Thomas, "Another time Jesus went forth into the street, and a boy running by, rushed upon his shoulder; at which Jesus, being angry, said to him, thou shalt go no farther. And he instantly fell down dead" (The Gospel of Thomas 2:7-9). The Gospel of Thomas concludes with these words, "Simon Peter said to them, 'Mary, leave us, for women are not worthy of life.' Jesus said, 'I myself shall lead her in order to make her male, so that she too may become a living spirit resembling you males. For every woman who will make herself male will enter the kingdom of heaven" (The Gospel of Thomas 114).

Bruce makes the interesting observation, "It is remarkable, when one comes to think of it, that the four canonical Gospels are anonymous, whereas the 'Gospels' which proliferated in the late second century and afterward claimed to have been written by apostles and other eyewitnesses. Catholic churchmen found it necessary, therefore, to defend the apostolic authenticity of the Gospels, which they accepted against the claims of those which they rejected. Hence come the accounts of the origin of the canonical four which appear in the Muratorian list, in the so-called anti-Marcionite prologues, and in Irenaeus" (Bruce, CS, p. 257).

To summarize, in the third and fourth centuries, certain canonical books were doubted, and others were rejected. It should be noted that thirty-four books in the Old Testament and twenty in the New Testament have little or no dispute (Baker, p. 84).

"Passing disagreement on a few books should not be allowed to overshadow in importance a greater measure of agreement on the majority of the books. Furthermore, basic agreement on the canon by various sections of the church on a voluntary basis (apart from and prior to action by church councils) is a noteworthy fact that should be given its full weight" (Everett Harrison, p. 113).

Are there lost books of the Bible? Ryrie says, "Even if a letter of Paul were discovered, it would not be canonical. After all, Paul must have written many letters during his lifetime in addition to the ones that are in the New Testament, yet the church did not include them in the canon. Not everything an apostle wrote was inspired, for it was not the writer who was inspired but his writings, and not necessarily all of them" (Ryrie, p. 106).

Conclusion

What conclusions can be drawn after looking at the available data from both inside and outside the Bible?

From the Scriptures themselves, it is apparent that in the case of the Law (the five books of Moses), the Prophets (the rest of the Old Testament), the Gospels (four books), and the epistles (the remainder of the New Testament), God spoke, men wrote what God spoke or what He moved them to write, and God influenced people so that they took note that what was written was the Word of God. It is also evident that many other books were written during the Old Testament period. By the time Luke wrote, many other gospels had already been written (Lk. 1:1-4), and during the lifetime of the Apostle Paul, letters were written in his name (2 Thess. 2:2). Therefore, a selection process was in place.

Based on what Jesus said about the Scripture and the doctrine of inspiration, it is reasonable to believe that God inspired His Word for people beyond the original recipients. He providentially worked to ensure that His Word was recognized. Inspiration and canonization are the work of God. He is the One who determined which books were included and which were excluded. That is the traditional evangelical view.

The canon does not derive its authority from the sanction of Jewish priests and leaders or the Christian Church. That authority is in itself. The collection of the canon is merely the assembling into one volume of those books whose sacred character and claim have already secured general acknowledgment (Unger, pp. 73-74).

At the end of his book on the canon, Bruce says, "The theological aspect of canonization has not been the subject of this book, which has been concerned rather with the historical aspect, but for those who receive the scriptures as God's Word written, the theological aspect is the most important" (Bruce, CS, p. 281). He adds, "The work of the Holy Spirit is not discerned by means of the common tools of the historian's trade. His inner witness gives the assurance to hearers or readers of scripture that, in its words, God himself is addressing them, but when one is considering the process by which the canon of scripture took shape, it would be wiser to speak of the providence or guidance of the Spirit than of his witness" (Bruce, CS, p. 281).

William Barclay says, "The New Testament books became canonical because no one could stop them doing so." Cullmann says, "The books which were to form the future canon forced themselves on the Church by their intrinsic apostolic authority, as they do still because the Kyrios Christ speaks in them" (Cullmann, cited by Bruce, CS, p. 282).

Ancient authors were aware of the inspiration of the Scripture. Clement of Rome said Paul wrote to the Corinthians "under the inspiration of the Spirit" (1 Clement 47:1-3). Irenaeus makes it clear that the Scriptures, even when they are not clearly understood, "were spoken by the Word of God and by His Spirit" (Irenaeus, Haer. 2.28.2). Theophilus of Antioch (ca. 180) asserts, "The holy writings teach us, and all the spirit-bearing ... that at first God was alone, and Word in Him" (Theophilus, Autol. 2.22). Inspiration involved "men of God carrying in them a holy spirit and becoming prophets, being inspired and made wise by God, became God-taught, and holy and righteous" (Theophilus, Autol. 2:9). Origen maintained that "the Scriptures were written by the Spirit of God" (Irenaeus, First Principles preface 8). Seeking to discredit the Doctrine of Peter, he says that he can show that it was not written by Peter "or by any other person inspired by the Spirit of God" (First Principles preface 8). The operating assumption here, of course, is that Scripture is inspired, but heresy and falsehood are not.

The "Festal Letter" of Athanasius (AD 367) distinguishes sharply between "God-inspired Scripture ... handed down to our fathers by those who were eyewitnesses and servants of the word from the beginning" and the "so-called secret writings" of heretics. Athanasius' list comprised the four Gospels, Acts, James, I and II Peter, I, II, and III John, Jude, Romans, I and II Corinthians, Galatians, Ephesians, Philippians, Colossians, I and II Thessalonians, Hebrews, I and II Timothy, Titus, Philemon, and Revelation. "These," said Athanasius, "are springs of salvation ...

let no one add to them or take away from them." Note: he listed the twenty-seven books of the New Testament.

Modern scholars have acknowledged that the issue in canonization is inspiration. Westcott "emphasized the importance of a superintending providence guiding the church from the beginning to an appreciation of the books that time and use confirmed" (Everett Harrison, p. 107). Concerning the canon, Westcott writes, "Its limits were fixed in the earliest times by use rather than by criticism; and this use itself was based on immediate knowledge" (Westcott, p. 496). Again, he affirms that it was under the influence of the Spirit that the church recognized in the New Testament the law of its constitution (Westcott, p. 498). The formation of the canon was an act of the intuition of the church (Westcott, p. 498).

Karl Barth states, "In no sense of the concept could or can the Church give the Canon to itself. The Church cannot 'form' it, as historians have occasionally said, without being aware of the theological implications. The Church can only confirm or establish it as something which has already been formed and given" (Karl Barth, *Church Dogmatics* I/2, p. 473).

As Tenney concludes, canonicity cannot be determined by authorship nor by the church's acceptance. "The church did not determine the canon; it recognized the canon" (Tenney, p. 421). "The true criterion of canonicity is inspiration" (Tenney, p. 418). As Tenney explains, if inspiration is the essential quality of canonicity, no council could create a canon because no group could not inspire what was already inspired! All any council could do is give their opinion concerning which books were canonical and let history justify or reverse their verdict (Tenney, p. 421).

Summary: Inspiration determines canonicity. God inspired His Word and saw to it that it was recognized as His Word.

Here is a succinct summary. The Bible claims to be the Word of God (2 Tim. 3:16). Beginning with Moses, God spoke to men who wrote what God said to them or God moved them to write (2 Pet. 1:21). Both the Old Testament and the New Testament record there was an immediate recognition that what was written was the Word of God (Dan. 9:2; 1 Tim. 5:18; 2 Pet 3:15-16).

In the case of the Old Testament, there are indications outside the Bible that the prophets ceased after the last book of the Old Testament was written (Josephus, etc.). The New Testament, in general, and Jesus, in particular, refer to the Old Testament as if it were a closed canon (see Lk. 11:50-51; 24:44).

In the case of the New Testament, what can be said about information outside the Bible is as follows:

1. Immediately after the last book of the New Testament was written (AD 95), books of the New Testament were known and used as authority, and some were called inspired (1 Clement does that).

2. During the second century, the books of the New Testament were recognized as Scripture, and there are indications that there was a canon. There is no list of all the books in the New Testament, but by the end of the second century, there is evidence that the four Gospels, Acts, the epistles of Paul, 1 Peter, 1 John, and Revelation, were recognized as canonical Scripture (Irenaeus). Most churches at the end of the second century were in basic agreement with the core of Irenaeus' collection of New Testament books (McDonald, p. 298). In fact, Westcott says, "From the time of Irenaeus, the New Testament was composed essentially of the same books which we receive at present, and

that they were regarded with the same reverence as is now shown to them" (Westcott, p. 6).

3. In the third and fourth centuries, some doubted some of the books in the New Testament, and during this time, some of the non-canonical books were declared spurious (see statements by Origen and Eusebius).

4. In the fourth century, there was formal recognition of what the church had already recognized.

Chapter 5

It Is Reasonable To Believe God's Message Is Accurate: Part 2

If the 66 books of the Bible contain God's message, the next question is, "Do we have an accurate copy of what was originally written?" The Old Testament was originally handwritten in Hebrew, with a few chapters in Aramaic. The New Testament was handwritten initially in Greek. These original manuscripts no longer exist. However, they were copied, and those copies were copied, and those copies were copied, until the invention of the printing press. The copies that exist today do not always agree with each other. So, how do we know which manuscripts are the most accurate?

This issue has caused some to reject the Bible and Christianity. Wallace said that when he was an atheist, this issue "was one of my prime complaints about the Bible" (Wallace, p. 101). In his opinion, this problem "invalidated the evidential value of the text altogether" (Wallace, p. 107). Is it reasonable to believe that God's message in the Bible is accurate?

The Text of the Old Testament

The Jews meticulously copied the Hebrew Old Testament, as well as the small Aramaic portions within it. They did things such as counting each letter on a page, copying the page, and then counting the letters on the copy to ensure they had the correct number. As a result, we no doubt have a very reliable copy of the original Old Testament today.

Masoretic Text By the sixth century AD, a group of textual scholars named "Masoretes," a Hebrew word derived from the Hebrew word for "tradition," continued to preserve the Old Testament Scriptures. The text they produced became known as the Masoretic text, which became the officially recognized text of the Hebrew Bible (Farstad, p. 94).

Until the mid-20th century, the oldest known copy of the Hebrew Old Testament was a Masoretic Text dated to approximately AD 900. Then, the Dead Sea Scrolls were discovered. Among the Dead Sea Scrolls was a copy of Isaiah, dated between 100 and 200 BC. In other words, with the discovery of the Isaiah scroll, we jumped 1000 years closer to when the original Hebrew manuscript of Isaiah was written.

The differences between the Isaiah manuscript of the Masoretic Text and the Isaiah manuscript of the Dead Sea Scrolls are few and minor. In a few places, there are differences regarding aspects such as the presence or absence of an article or the distinction between singular and plural forms. That's incredible! If that is true for the Isaiah manuscript, it is no doubt true of the remainder of the Masoretic Text of the Old Testament. There is little doubt that we have an accurate copy of the Hebrew Old Testament.

Other Sources There are, however, a few problems. In some places, the text in the Old Testament is obscure. On occasion, there is a word that appears only once in all of the Old Testament. Other versions of the Old Testament exist. The Samaritans had a version of the Pentateuch that differed from the Masoretic Text in certain places. There was also a Greek translation of the Old Testament, known as the Septuagint (also referred to as the LXX), which was completed around 250 BC.

Some modern English translations closely follow the Traditional Text of the Old Testament, that is, the Masoretic Text. Others practice emendation, which involves altering the Masoretic Text based on other sources. These differences are minor. No major issue is affected.

The Text of the New Testament

There are over six thousand handwritten manuscripts of the Greek New Testament. The vast, vast majority of those manuscripts form one category. That category of manuscripts has been called the Textus Receptus (Latin for "received text"), the Syrian Text, the Traditional Text, the Majority Text, and the Byzantine Text.

In the 19th century, two Greek manuscripts were found, one in the monastery at the foot of Mount Sinai and the other in the Vatican. At the time, those two manuscripts (Sinaiticus and Vaticanus) were dated earlier than any of the manuscripts in the majority category. That category has been called the Alexandrian Text because those two manuscripts were from Egypt.

In my book, *The New Testament Greek Issue*, I explained in detail the differences between these two categories of manuscripts. It is available on Amazon and Barnes & Noble, and at a discount on my website at www.insightsfromtheword.com. Here is a simple explanation of the situation.

First, no central doctrine of Christianity is affected. All scholars agree with that. Except for fragments that do not address these issues, all extant New Testament Greek manuscripts teach the doctrine of the Trinity, the deity of Christ, the death and resurrection of Jesus Christ, salvation by grace through faith, and other related teachings.

Second, the primary difference between the two categories of manuscripts lies in the fact that the Alexandrian Text tends to omit passages and verses found in the Byzantine Text. For example, the Alexandrian Text omits the last 12 verses of Mark (Mk. 16:9-20), the story of the woman taken in adultery (Jn. 7:53-8:11), the ending of the Lord's Prayer (Mt. 6:13), and the phrase "in Ephesus" (Eph. 1:1), among others.

Third, the King James Version and the New King James Version are based on the Byzantine Text. The well-known English translations of the 20th century are based on the Alexandrian Text, such as the NASB, the NIV, and the ESV.

Fourth, the vast majority of Greek manuscripts were produced between approximately AD 500 and AD 1200. Sinaiticus and Vaticanus are from the middle of the fourth century (AD 350). So, the whole debate comes down to this: *the many, which are considered to be late, versus the few, which are earlier.*

The question is, "Which type of text is closest to what was initially written by the authors of the New Testament? Isn't the answer that earlier manuscripts are closer to the original? Not necessarily. Remember the Dead Sea Scrolls of Isaiah. The late 9th-century Masoretic Text of Isaiah proved to be remarkably close to a manuscript of Isaiah that was 1,000 years earlier.

The Byzantine Text

1. The Area of Origin. The Byzantine text type originates from the area where almost all the autographs were originally written or where they were sent. Therefore, they were the first to be copied. Byzantium was the name given to the eastern part of the Roman Empire. Sixteen books of the New Testament were either written from or to that area: Matthew, John, Galatians, Ephesians, Colossians, 1 and 2 Timothy, Philemon, 1 and 2 Peter, 1, 2, 3 John, Revelation, and probably James and Jude. Six books of the New Testament were written to Greece: 1 and 2 Corinthians, Philippians, 1 and 2 Thessalonians, and Titus, who was in Crete. Five books of the New Testament were connected with Rome, including Mark, Romans, probably Luke, Acts, and possibly Hebrews. In other words, 22 of the 27 books of the New Testament were either written from or to Asia Minor or Greece. The other five pertain to Rome.

2. Copied. The autographs were copied immediately, even before the New Testament was completed. Paul expected his writings to be read beyond the churches to which they were sent (1 Thess. 5:27; Col. 4:16; see "the churches of Galatia" in Gal. 1:2; "all the saints in Achaia" in 2 Cor. 1:1; "all who in every place" in 1 Cor. 1:2). John intended the same thing (Rev. 1:1-3; see "churches," plural in 2:7, 2:11, 2:17, 2:29; 3:6, 3:13, 3:22). So did Peter (1 Pet. 1:1). Peter calls Paul's letters Scripture and speaks about them to a group of churches in such a way that indicates they had seen copies of them (2 Peter 3:15-16). "Copies of the original would be made for use in neighboring churches. The circulation of a book would be like the rippling of the stone cast into a pond, spreading out in all directions at once" (Aland, p. 55).

3. Carefully Copied. From the beginning, those who received the Scriptures were warned not to mishandle them. Moses cautioned, "You shall not add to the word which I command you, nor take from it, that you may keep the commandments of the LORD your God which I command you" (Deut. 4:2). Later, he repeated the caution, "Whatever I command you, be careful to observe it; you shall not add to it nor take away from it" (Deut. 12:32). Proverbs echoes the admonition, "Every word of God is pure; He is a shield to those who put their trust in Him. Do not add to His words, Lest He rebuke you, and you be found a liar" (Prov. 30:5-6). The Old Testament saints were taught not to change the Scriptures.

"Josephus confirms that the Old Testament principle ... continued to be recognized in the first century" (Kruger, p. 72). Josephus wrote, "We have given practical proof of our reverence for our own Scripture. Therefore, although such long ages have now passed, no one has ventured either to add or to remove, or to alter a syllable" (Ag. Ap. 1.42).

The Old Testament text found among the Dead Sea Scrolls is virtually identical to the medieval Masoretic texts, demonstrating textual consistency over centuries. For example, 4QGen, a manuscript of Genesis 1:1-28 (dated to the 1st century AD), is identical to the Masoretic text (dated to AD 1008) except for one spelling variant. The differences between the Masoretic text of Isaiah and the one found in the Dead Sea Scrolls are exceedingly minor, such as spelling differences (like "colour" in England versus "color" in America) and the addition of a single letter (the Hebrew letter ו, which is translated "and").

4. Early Existence. The Byzantine text type existed early in Greek manuscripts, translations, and the writings of Christians.

It is Reasonable To Believe God Has Message Is Accurate: Part 2

5. The Majority of the Manuscripts. The Byzantine Text is the text type of 80 to 95 percent of all Greek manuscripts (Farstad, p. 109). The question is, how does one explain the fact that the vast majority of manuscripts support the majority text type? The Declaration of Independence was written in 1776. Suppose there was no printing press at that time and people began to copy the Declaration of Independence by hand. Then, imagine that around 1820, someone made a copy that contained changes that began to be copied. All things being equal, which document would produce the most manuscripts today: the original 1776 document or the copy that was changed in 1820?

6. Unity. The Byzantine text type contains remarkable unity. In fact, the majority of Greek manuscripts display more uniformity than the Vulgate, an official fourth-century edition of the Latin manuscripts by Jerome. That's incredible! The majority of Greek manuscripts consist of a smooth Greek text with no grammatical, historical, or geographical errors. "The very smoothness and completeness of the text led these scholars (Westcott and Hort) to believe it (the Syrian text type) was late, edited, and hence corrupt" (Farstad, p. 108). Sinaiticus and Vaticanus do not have such uniformity and contain mistakes (see below).

7. Use. The Byzantine text type has been used throughout the centuries. That's why it's called the Traditional Text. "All modern critics acknowledge that this [Byzantine text type] was the Greek New Testament text in general use throughout the greater part of the Byzantine Period (312-1453)" (Hills, Introduction, p. 20). Did God hide the best manuscripts of the New Testament until 1859?

8. Divine Preservation. The Byzantine text type is the only text type that has been continually preserved. Several verses say that God would preserve His Word (Mt. 5:18; 24:35; Mk. 13:31;

Lk. 16:17; 21:33; 1 Pet. 1:24-25). Did God preserve His Word through the centuries? If He did, then the Byzantine Text must be closer to the original because it was continually preserved. This argument will not appeal to everyone. It will only appeal to people who believe in the inspiration and the preservation of the Word of God. But as one Greek professor said, "To what better kind of person would you want to appeal?"

Alexandrian Text

The Alexandrian text came from Egypt. "As far as we know, not a single original autograph of a Gospel or Epistle was ever sent to Egypt" (Farstad, p. 110). It has been suggested that Sinaiticus and Vaticanus "represent a local text which never had any significant currency except in that part of the ancient world. By contrast, most manuscripts were widely diffuse, and their ancestral roots must have reached back to the autographs themselves (Hodges and Farstad, p. x).

The Alexandrian text contains mistakes. In Matthew 1, the genealogy of Christ in Vaticanus and Sinaiticus lists two non-existent kings. They list "Asaph" instead of "Asa" (Mt. 1:7) and "Amos" instead of Amon" (Mt. 1:10). In the Old Testament, there was a prophet named Amos and a musician named Asaph, but they were not kings in the Messianic line (Farstad, p. 115; Borland, pp. 499-506).

In Matthew 6:13, the doxology at the end of the Lord's prayer, "For Yours is the kingdom and the power and the glory forever. Amen," is not in Sinaiticus and Vaticanus. It is in Luke, the Didache—a document that many believe was written before AD 100—and in translations of the New Testament, which were much earlier than the fourth century. Without the doxology, the prayer concludes with the words "evil" or "evil one," which seems odd, especially because it is traditional to end a Jewish prayer with praise to God. Farstad asks, "Since most manuscripts do contain the ending, isn't it easier for Christians to believe that some manuscripts dropped off the ending simply by careless copying?" (Farstad, pp. 115-117).

Mark 16:9-20 are not in Sinaiticus and Vaticanus. In Vaticanus, there is a blank space for it, the only blank space in the whole manuscript, which means the scribe who was copying Vaticanus knew about the passage. Irenaeus (115?-202) cites Mark 16:9. Justin (100-165) echoes Mark 16:20.

If the Gospel of Mark ends with Mark 16:8, it concludes with the Greek word "gar" (meaning "for"), which would be abrupt and abnormal. "To end a book on this word seems most unlikely" (Farstad, p. 113). It is usually the second word in the sentence. Metzger says, "To terminate a Greek sentence with the word gar is most unusual and exceedingly rare—only a relative few examples have been found in all of the vast range of Greek literary works, and no instances have been found where gar stands at the end of the book. Moreover, it is possible that in verse 8, Mark uses the verb εφοβουντο to mean 'they were afraid of' (as he does in four of the other occurrences of this verb in his gospel). In that case, obviously, something is needed to finish the sentence" (Metzger, p. 228). Even Hort, who believes the book ends with verse 8, observes that it ends with "singular abruptness," adding that the sentence is not even complete. If Mark ends with Mark 16:8, it ends with the disciples being afraid (16:8). Can you imagine Mark doing that?

In his commentary on Mark, Hort says, "It cannot have been meant to conclude thus" either some accident may have prevented its completion, or a leaf of the original copy may have been lost." Alexander, the famous Princeton Theological Seminary professor of the 19th century, said that to suppose that Mark ends with verse 8 is "folly."

In Luke 23:45, Sinaiticus and Vaticanus contain a scientific mistake. Luke 23:45 says, "Then the sun was darkened, and the veil of the temple was torn in two," indicating an eclipse, but that is impossible because Christ died at Passover when the moon was full. The sun cannot be eclipsed during a full moon (Farstad, p. 115; see Borland's article mentioned above).

In John 7:53-8:11, the story of the woman taken in adultery is not in Sinaiticus and Vaticanus. Augustine wrote that it was omitted for fear it would promote immorality (Farstad, p. 113). The omission renders the grammar of the passage nonsensical. If John 7 stops at verse 52, the text of John reads, "They answered and said to him, 'Are you also from Galilee? Search and look, for no prophet has arisen out of Galilee'" (Jn. 7:52). "Then Jesus spoke to them again, saying, 'I am the light of the world. He who follows Me shall not walk in darkness, but have the light of life'" (Jn. 8:12). As Pickering explains, "What is the antecedent of 'them' and what is the meaning of 'again'? By the normal rules of grammar, if 7:53-8:11 is missing, then 'them' must refer to the 'Pharisees' and 'again' means that there has already been at least one prior exchange. But 7:45 makes clear that Jesus **was not there** with the Pharisees" (Pickering, pp. 329-330, bold print his). Such a construction of the text has Jesus addressing the meeting of Nicodemus and the Sanhedrin, but Jesus was not present at that meeting.

In Ephesians 1:1, the words "in Ephesus" are not in Sinaiticus and Vaticanus, but they are in 99.2% of all existing manuscripts of Ephesians.

In 1 Thessalonians 2:7, instead of the word "gentle," Sinaiticus and Vaticanus read the word "babies." In the Byzantine text, the verse reads, "But we were gentle among you, just as a nursing mother cherishes her own children." Sinaiticus and Vaticanus say, "But we were babes among you, just as a nursing mother cherishes her own children." In the Greek text, the only difference between the two words is that one has an "n" in front of it, and the other does not. Although the reading "We were babes among you" does not make sense because "babes" is in Vaticanus and Sinaiticus, which are older, some scholars argue that "babes" is the correct reading while admitting that "gentle" makes excellent sense (Lightfoot). Hiebert cites Mace, who says, "No manuscript is as old as common sense."

This is only a sample of the problems with Sinaiticus and Vaticanus. There are many, many more.

Summary: The geographical origin, majority, age, unity, and use throughout all of church history support the claim that the Byzantine text type is the best representation of the original text of the New Testament.

The point is that if the Bible is the Word of God, it is reasonable to believe that we have an accurate message. Remember, both types of text teach the central doctrines of Christianity. All extant New Testament Greek manuscripts teach the doctrine of the Trinity, the deity of Christ, the death and resurrection of Jesus Christ, and salvation by grace through faith, among other key Christian teachings.

In comparison to other written materials from the ancient world, the evidence for the New Testament is overwhelming.

Wallace says, "There are no better attested ancient documents than the New Testament Gospels. By way of comparison, the Greek researcher and historian Herodotus wrote The Histories in the fifth century BC. We trust that we have an accurate copy of this text, even though we possess only eight ancient copies. By comparison, we possess thousands of ancient copies of the New Testament documents. These copies come to us from all over the ancient world surrounding the Mediterranean" (Wallace, p. 235).

Chapter 6
God's Message To You

If God has revealed a message in the Bible to the people on planet Earth, what is the message?

The Message is about God

God's Attributes The Bible is, first and foremost, about God. Theologians described God by detailing His attributes. His attributes include sovereignty (1 Chron. 29:11-12), omnipresence (Ps. 139:7-12), immutability (Mal. 3:6), omniscience (1 Jn. 3:20), omnipotence (Rev. 19:6), holiness (Lev. 11:44), righteousness (Ezra 9:15), loving, (1 Jn. 4:8), gracious (Ps. 116:5), and faithfulness (1 Cor. 10:13).

As I have studied the Scriptures, I have been struck by the fact that while all of these attributes of God are mentioned repeatedly, the Old Testament emphasizes that God is holy (Lev. 11:44) and the New Testament stresses God is love (1 Jn. 4:8). Around holiness can be grouped such attributes as truth, righteousness, and justice; clustered about love are grace, mercy, and kindness. Thus, the two major attributes of God are holiness (truth, righteousness, justice) and love (grace, mercy, kindness).

Those two basic attributes are emphasized over and over again throughout the Scripture, in the **Pentateuch** (Ex. 34:5-8), in the **Psalms** (Ps. 108:4: "For Your mercy is great above the heavens, and Your truth reaches to the clouds;" this is one example of many), in the **Prophets** (Micah 6:8: "He has shown you, O man, what is good; and what does the LORD require of you but to do justly, to love mercy, and to walk humbly with your God?"), in the **Gospels** (in Mt.: 23:23: Jesus said, "the weightier matters of the law (are) justice and mercy and faith"), and in the **epistles** (Eph. 4:15: "speaking the truth in love").

God's Desire Simply put, God wants to be our God. What does it mean for God to be our God?

God desires to provide for His children. He told Moses, "Therefore say to the children of Israel: 'I am the LORD; **I will** bring you out from under the burdens of the Egyptians, **I will** rescue you from their bondage, and I will redeem you with an outstretched arm and with great judgments'" (Ex. 6:6). "**I will** take you as My people, and **I will** be your God. Then you shall know that I am the LORD your God who brings you out from under the burdens of the Egyptians" (Ex. 6:7). "And **I will** bring you into the land which I swore to give to Abraham, Isaac, and Jacob; and **I will** give it to you as a heritage: I am the LORD" (Ex. 6:6-8, bold type added). In these three verses, the Lord says "**I will**" seven times. These are the seven things that He will provide for them. These seven things are summarized in Leviticus. "I am the LORD your God, who brought you out of the land of Egypt, to give you the land of Canaan and to be your God" (Lev. 25:38). So, in short, God told Israel he wanted to redeem them (Ex. 6:6), be their God (Ex. 6:7), and give them the land of Canaan (Ex. 6:8). These are some of the things the Lord will provide for them.

They were no sooner out of Egypt than they began to complain (Ex. 16:2). Their complaint was that in Egypt they had "pots of meat" and bread to eat "to the full," but Moses brought us to the wilderness to kill us with starvation (Ex. 16:3). In response, the

Lord said, "I will rain bread from heaven" (Ex. 16:4). In fact, He provided "meat to eat in the evening and in the morning bread to the full" (Ex. 16:8).

Speaking to the Lord, David says in Psalm 65, "You visit the earth and water it, You greatly enrich it; the river of God is full of water; You provide their grain, for so You have prepared it" (Ps. 65:9). With rain provided by God, the earth is enriched, rivers are full, and grains grow. We give thanks before we eat because we recognize that God has provided the food.

God is still in the business of redeeming people. Paul says that in Christ, "We have redemption through His blood, the forgiveness of sins" (Col. 1:14). In other words, because Christ died for our sins and rose from the dead (1 Cor. 15:3), those who trust Him receive forgiveness of their sins and become the children of God (Jn. 1:12).

God is still in the business of providing for our needs. Jesus taught us to pray "give us this day our daily bread" (Mt. 6:11). "Therefore, I say to you, do not worry about your life, what you will eat or what you will drink; nor about your body, what you will put on. Is not life more than food and the body more than clothing? Look at the birds of the air, for they neither sow nor reap nor gather into barns; yet your heavenly Father feeds them. Are you not of more value than they? Which of you by worrying, can add one cubit to his stature? So why do you worry about clothing? Consider the lilies of the field, how they grow: they neither toil nor spin; and yet I say to you that even Solomon in all his glory was not arrayed like one of these. Now if God so clothes the grass of the field, which today is, and tomorrow is thrown into the oven, will He not much more clothe you, O you of little faith? Therefore, do not worry, saying, 'What shall we eat?' or 'What shall we drink?' or 'What shall we wear?' For after all these things the Gentiles seek. For your heavenly Father knows that you need all these things. But seek first the kingdom of God and His righteousness, and all these things shall be added to you. Therefore, do not worry about tomorrow, for tomorrow will worry about its own things. Sufficient for the day is its own trouble" (Mt. 6:25-34). That does not mean God delivers the food to our doorstep like Uber Eats. He supplies this need through our work. Paul said, "If anyone will not work, neither shall he eat" (2 Thess. 3:10).

God desires to protect His children. The Psalms repeatedly speak of the protection of the Lord. For example, "Keep me as the apple of Your eye; hide me under the shadow of Your wings, from the wicked who oppress me, from my deadly enemies who surround me" (Ps. 17:8-9). The Hebrew word translated "keep" means "to keep, guard." David asks the Lord to protect him like a bird protects its young under its wings. Other common figures in the Psalter are such things as a refuge, a shelter, and a fortress. "The LORD is your keeper; The LORD is your shade at your right hand. The sun shall not strike you by day, nor the moon by night. The LORD shall preserve you from all evil; He shall preserve your soul. The LORD shall preserve your going out and your coming in From this time forth, and even forevermore" (Ps. 121:5-8).

God wants to prosper His children. The Lord prospered Israel by giving them a land flowing with milk and honey. That expression appears in the Old Testament 20 times (Ex. 3:8. 17; 13:5; 33:3; Lev. 20:24; Num. 13:27; 14:8; 16:13-14; Deut. 6:3; 11:9; 26:9, 15; 27:3; 31:20; Jos. 5:6; Jer. 11:5; 32:22; Ezek. 20:6; 20:15). In Exodus 3:8, the land flowing with milk and honey is called "a good and large land." In Ezekiel 20:6 and 20:15, it is said to be "the glory of all lands." "Blessed is the man who walks not in the counsel of the ungodly, nor stands in the path of sinners, Nor sits in the seat of the scornful, but his delight is in the law of the LORD, and in His law he meditates day and night. He shall be like a tree planted by the rivers of water, that brings forth its fruit in its season, whose leaf also shall not wither; And whatever he does shall prosper" (Ps. 1:1-3).

To sum up, God wants to be our God, which means He wants to provide, protect, and prosper us.

The Message is about People

God's message is not only about Himself; it is also about people. What does God have to say about people? The biblical teaching on humanity is typically divided into two major parts: dignity and depravity.

Dignity When God created people, He said, "Let us make man in our image, according to Our likeness" (Gen. 1:26). The Hebrew word translated "image" means "image, likeness, resemblance." The word translated "likeness" means "likeness or similitude." The second phrase is merely supplementary or explanatory of the first. Therefore, they do not refer to two different things. The two words are used interchangeably to express the idea that people were created in the very image of God. God made people not only according to His plan but according to the pattern of His own person.

Coins are stamped from a die. When you examine a coin, you can tell what was engraved in the die because the coin bears the image of the die that pressed it. Likewise, people bear the resemblance of God. The question is, "What is the likeness?"

The phrase "the image of God" does not include the body, for God is spirit (Jn. 4:24) and a spirit does not have flesh and bones (Lk. 24:39). God is invisible (Col. 1:15). Remember also that God forbade images for the simple reason that there was nothing in the earth that could resemble Him (Deut. 4:15-19).

If the image of God in people does not include the body, what does it include? Theologians have debated this question for centuries. One of the most common suggestions is that since God is holy and people have His image, they have the capacity for holiness. There appears to be support for this view in Ephesians 4:24. Following salvation, the new person is created in righteousness and true holiness, after God's own image.

Whether or not Ephesians 4:24 proves that the image of God in people is the capacity for holiness, this much is certain. Before the fall, Adam had fellowship with God, but the animals did not. Adam was a spiritual being with spiritual capacities.

Even if the capacity for holiness view is correct, it does not explain everything. After the Fall, people retained the image of God, at least to some degree (Gen. 9:6; 2 Cor. 11:7), but after the Fall, people were not holy. Therefore, to say that the image is holiness does not tell the whole story.

That observation has driven many to the conclusion that the image involves personhood, that is, God is a person (a being with mind, emotions, and will), and, thus, when people were created in His image, they, too, had intellectual power, natural affection, and moral freedom. They at least had sufficient intelligence to give names to all the animals (Gen. 2:19-20). Adam could think, reason, and speak. He could attach words to ideas. Humans did not lose these capacities after the Fall. Colossians 3:10 seems to support this view. After salvation, the new person is created in the knowledge of God, in the image of God who created them.

The image of God in people, then, is not physical but spiritual and primarily in His personhood. Children are often said to be "just like" their father or mother. That can be physical, such as the features of their face, but it can also be non-physical, like their personality. I have children, all of whom have various things about them that are exactly like me. The one characteristic people comment about the most is that one of them has my personality. It is often said, "Your oldest daughter is just like you." She is outgoing, fun-loving, and talks a lot. She is made in my image, but that is not physical; it is non-physical.

A definition of the doctrine of the dignity of people is: Humans were created in the image of God and, thus, have a capacity for holiness and personality (Gen. 1:26; Eph. 4:24; Col. 3:10).

People are made in the image of God, an image which remains, at least to some degree, even after Adam sinned. People have dignity. The Bible applies this truth in two specific areas. It tells us that since people are created in the image of God, they should not commit murder (Gen. 9:6), nor should they slander (Jas. 3:9). Since people are made in the image of God, they should not destroy one another, either with a gun or with gossip.

The biblical view of you is that you are made in the image of God and, therefore, have dignity. Some people think too lowly of themselves. Because of the way they have been treated or the way they have behaved, they think of themselves as worthless worms. You have worth and dignity; you have been created in the image of God.

Depravity The second major thing the Bible teaches about people is that they are sinful; they are depraved. What does that mean? How depraved is this depravity?

Depravity does not mean that people have no knowledge of God or righteousness (Rom. 2:14-15), nor that people are as sinful as they can be (2 Tim. 3:13). It does not even mean that people commit every possible type of sin (Mt. 23:23). In fact, some sins rule out other sins. Pride prohibits some people from committing other sins. Depravity does not even mean that people can never do good works. Most people honor their parents. Even killers do not kill everyone, which is a good thing.

Depravity means people lost their holiness in the Fall (Adam's disobedience). They are now unholy, unrighteous, and ungodly (Rom. 5:12, 19; 3:10, 23). Depravity also means that every part of people was affected by the Fall. Humans now have a darkened mind (2 Cor. 4:4), degraded emotions (Jer. 17:9), and a disobedient will (Rom. 3:11; Isa. 53:6).

Consider Paul's description of unbelievers in Ephesians. "This I say, therefore, and testify in the Lord, that you should no longer walk as the rest of the Gentiles walk, in the futility of their mind, having their understanding darkened, being alienated from the life of God, because of the ignorance that is in them, because of the hardness of their heart; who, being past feeling, have given themselves over to lewdness, to work all uncleanness with greediness" (Eph. 4:17-19). Notice, the references to mind ("the futility of their mind," the "understanding darkened"), emotions ("hardness of their heart," "past feeling") and will ("given themselves," "to work").

The same thing can be seen in Titus. "For we ourselves were also once foolish, disobedient, deceived, serving various lusts and pleasures, living in malice and envy, hateful and hating one another" (Titus 3:3). Again, notice the references to mind ("foolish" means "no understanding"), emotions ("lust and pleasures"), and will ("disobedient," "living in malice").

To say the same thing another way, people react emotionally, think irrationally, act irresponsibly, blame others, play victim, and if you tell them the truth, they throw stones at you.

Stanley Collins, an English preacher, tells of the time as a small lad when he had a half-cent piece, which is the size of an American quarter, and needed a whole cent, an English coin the size of a half-dollar. A friend suggested that he put it on the rail of a streetcar, which he did. After the train passed over it, the side with the head of the king of England was still there, but the image had been destroyed. Humans are like that coin. They had the image of the king impressed and implanted in them, but the Fall destroyed it. It can still faintly be seen, but it has been destroyed.

To sum up, humans were created in the image of God and, thus, have dignity, but because of the Fall, they are depraved. Every part of them has been affected by sin.

If we have the same view of ourselves that God does, we understand that although we have dignity, we are depraved. We will not think too lowly of ourselves, as if we had no worth, nor will we think too highly of ourselves because we are depraved.

The Message is about Relationships

The Bible is about relationships, people's relationship with God, and people's relationship with one another

With God People do not automatically have a relationship with God. In the first three chapters of Romans, Paul explains the problem in detail. He concludes, "All have sinned and come short of the glory of God" (Rom. 3:23). John says, "sin is lawlessness" (1 Jn. 3:4). We have all broken God's law, that is, the 10 Commandments. That does not mean that we have broken all of the laws, but as James points out, "For whoever shall keep the whole law, and yet stumble in one point, he is guilty of all" (Jas, 2:8).

As there is a penalty for breaking the law of the state, so there is a penalty for breaking God's law, namely, death, which is spiritual separation from God. Paul declares, "The wages of sin is death" (Rom. 6:23).

Even though we have all sinned against God and deserve to be separated from God, God loves us and desires to have a relationship with us. So He sent His son to die in our place to pay for our sins. This is the most incredible, most amazing, life-changing truth in the Bible. "For when we were still without strength, in due time, Christ died for the ungodly. For scarcely for a righteous man will one die, yet perhaps for a good man, someone would even dare to die. But God demonstrates His own love toward us, in that while we were still sinners, Christ died for us" (Rom. 5:6-8). "Christ died for our sins according to the Scriptures … was buried, and … rose again the third day according to the Scriptures" (1 Cor. 15:3-4). In dying in our place to pay for our sins and being raised from the dead, Jesus Christ did everything necessary for us to be forgiven, have a relationship with God, and go to heaven when we die.

To illustrate, imagine we were in my car together when I was stopped for speeding and given a fine of $500. If I had to appear in court and could not pay the fine, and you were kind enough to pay it for me, how much would I owe the court? The answer, of course, is nothing. Likewise, my sin debt before God is "death." Jesus paid it when He died in my place to pay for my sin. So my debt is paid.

To have that kind of relationship with God, a person must trust Jesus Christ for the gift of eternal life (Rom. 6:23 says, "The gift of God is eternal life"). One of the most famous verses in the Bible says, "For God so loved the world that He gave His only begotten Son, that whoever believes in Him should not perish but have everlasting life" (Jn, 3:16). One must believe Jesus is the Son of God, who died to pay for sin and rose from the dead. This belief is more than believing about Jesus Christ. It is believing "on Him for everlasting life " (1 Tim. 1:16). When the Bible says believe "in Him" (Jn. 316) or "on Him" (1 Tim. 1:16; Acts 16:31), it indicates "trust Him" (Abbott-Smith and Arndt and Gingrich Greek lexicons). Believing in Jesus "for" eternal life, not just believing about Him. In other words, it is depending on Him to obtain forgiveness and the gift of eternal life.

It is essential to recognize that this involves trusting Jesus Christ, not any actions we take. Paul says, "For by grace you have been saved through faith, and that not of yourselves; it is the gift of God, not of works, lest anyone should boast" (Eph. 2:8-9). Salvation is a gift. It is not based on anything we do. It is based solely and only on Jesus Christ and what He did. He died for sin and rose from the dead.

It is now time to make a decision. Based on the evidence presented thus far, what is your decision? Is it reasonable to believe that there is a powerful, intelligent, personal God (Chapter 1)? Assuming that is a reasonable conclusion, then is it reasonable to believe that an intelligent, personal God has communicated to us? Based on fulfilled prophecy, the resurrection of Jesus Christ, and the personal experiences of millions of people over the last 2,000 years, is it reasonable to believe that God has communicated to us through the Bible (Chapter 2)? Based on historical evidence as well as the claim that God was involved in the writing of the Bible, is it reasonable to believe that we have an accurate message of what God says to us in the Bible (Chapters 3 and 4)? However, believing that there is a powerful, intelligent, personal God who has communicated to us through the Bible is not enough to ensure one's entry into heaven.

The issue is, have you trusted Jesus Christ for eternal life? Do you know for sure that when you die, you will go to heaven? Here is the test. If you stand before God and God asks you, "Why should I let you into heaven, what would you say? If you respond that you should be allowed to enter heaven because of Jesus (you "believe on Him;" or you "trust Him, who died for you and rose from the dead), you will be ushered into heaven. If you point to anything you have done, you will not be allowed to enter heaven. By the way, it is not about trusting Jesus plus something you do. It is trusting Jesus and Him alone, and nothing else.

Once people trust Jesus Christ, the Bible says they have been "born again," that is, they have been born spiritually (Jn. 3:7). They are called spiritual babies (Heb. 5:13). As physical babies need to grow to adulthood, so spiritual babies need to grow to spiritual maturity (Eph. 4:11-16). Peter explains how to do that when he says, "Therefore, laying aside all malice, all deceit, hypocrisy, envy, and all evil speaking, as newborn babes, desire the pure milk of the word, that you may grow thereby, if indeed you have tasted that the Lord is gracious" (1 Pet. 2:1-3). Believers are able to set aside sin and seek to obey the Word of God by depending upon the Spirit of God (Gal. 5:16). To grow, believers must obey the Word of God (1 Pet. 2:1-3), depend on the Spirit of God (Gal. 5:16), and fellowship with the people of God (Eph. 4:11-16). The goal of spiritual growth is Christ-like spiritual maturity, which involves being righteous and loving (Eph. 4:15-5:2).

Righteousness without love is judgmental. Love without righteousness is sentimentality. Being Christ-like is being both righteous and loving. These two things are not mutually exclusive. What is right is loving and what is truly loving is right.

With Others The Bible is also about people's relationships with one another. For example, the 10 Commandments address relationships with God (Commandments 1-4) and with one another (Commandments 5-10). Paul explains that all of that is fulfilled by simply loving one another. He says, "Owe no one anything except to love one another, for he who loves another has fulfilled the law. For the commandments, 'You shall not commit adultery,' 'You shall not murder,' 'You shall not steal,' 'You shall not bear false witness,' 'You shall not covet,' and if there is any other commandment, are all summed up in this saying, namely, 'You shall love your neighbor as yourself.' Love does no harm to a neighbor; therefore, love is the fulfillment of the law" (Rom. 13:8-10).

John put it like this, "In this, the love of God was manifested toward us, that God has sent His only begotten Son into the world, that we might live through Him. In this is love, not that we loved God, but that He loved us and sent His Son to be the propitiation for our sins. Beloved, if God so loved us, we also ought to love one another. No one has seen God at any time. If we love one another, God abides in us, and His love has been perfected (matured) in us" (1 Jn. 4:9-12).

Summary: God's message is about Him, us, and relationships. Christianity is not about religion; it is about relationships.

Unfortunately, when many think of Christianity, they think of religion, meaning participating in rituals and living by rules and regulations. Granted, there are things believers do, such as gathering together to hear the Scripture taught and to observe the Lord's Supper, but that is not the essence of Christianity. Believers do those things because they love God and each other. Granted, there are things believers do not do, that is, things the Scripture says are sins, but again, they are not living by rules and regulations. They are doing and not doing things because of their love for the Lord and each other.

Chapter 7
Conclusion

Is it reasonable to believe that God exists, that He has sent us a message, and that we have an accurate record of that message? The question is not, "Is it possible to 'prove' these things scientifically because the scientific method, which requires repeatability, is not applicable to these kinds of issues. However, it is logical to believe these things because if the premises are true, the logical conclusion must be true. In that sense, it is reasonable to believe.

The first premise is that, at the beginning, some form of life had to exist. That premise is true because the other possibilities, namely, that at the beginning there was nothing or that the material universe is eternal, are not true. Nothing cannot produce something. That eliminates that possibility. The design of the universe indicates an intelligent designer. That eliminates the possibility that the material universe is eternal. Therefore, at the beginning, there was some form of life. The nature of the universe indicates that this form of life had to possess unimaginable power, intelligence to produce order and design, and the will to create life. The name given to such life is God.

If the premise that there is a powerful, intelligent, personal God is true, it is reasonable to believe that such a God has communicated with us. The evidence that God has done so is the Bible, which is unlike any other book ever written. Its content demonstrates that it is a supernatural book. It predicts that the Messiah would be a man, a Jew, from the tribe of Judah, from the family of David, from the city of Bethlehem, from a virgin, the Son of God, who would die and be resurrected at a specific time. Those and other predictions were perfectly fulfilled in the coming of Jesus Christ. There is nothing like this in the history of the world. Other ancient and modern predictions give only one or two particulars expressed in general and ambiguous terms. Throughout all history, there is not a single instance of a prediction, expressed in unequivocal language, which has been fulfilled—except those found in the Scripture.

What the Bible does in predicting the coming of the Messiah would be like someone in the year 2000 predicting who would be President of the United States in the year 2050. They couldn't predict his family name and the city in which he was born, much less all the other predictions the Scripture gives concerning the coming of the Messiah.

If the premise that God was involved in the writing of the Bible is true, it is reasonable to believe that God saw to it that the right books were put in it and that the right text of it was preserved. From the very beginning of the Bible and throughout, God spoke, the men wrote, and people took note that what was written was the Word of God.

What Jesus said about the books we call the Old Testament (Luke 24:44) indicates that we have the correct books in the Old Testament. Paul cited a quotation from Luke (1 Timothy 5:18), referring to it as Scripture. Peter acknowledged that Paul wrote Scripture (1 Peter 5:15), and what he said (2 Peter 5:16) indicates that there was already a collection of what Paul wrote.

Summary: It is reasonable to believe that God exists, that God has communicated to us by being involved in writing the

Conclusion

Bible, and that we have an accurate copy of His message.

The essence of this approach is that if a premise is true, the logical conclusion must be true. In this case, the conclusion of the first premise (God) becomes the second premise, and the conclusion of the second premise (the Bible) becomes the third premise (an accurate copy of God's message).

It is one thing to believe that there is a God; it is another thing to have a personal relationship with God. It is one thing to believe that the Bible is the Word of God and that we have an accurate copy of it; it is another thing to have a personal relationship with the Lord. To have a relationship with the God of the Bible, you must believe that Jesus, the Son of God, died to pay for your sins and rose from the dead and then trust Him to give you eternal life, which means you are forgiven of your sins and will go to heaven when you die.

It all boils down to this: if you were to stand before God and He were to ask you, "Why should I let you into heaven?" What would you say? There are two possibilities: either you will tell Him about something you have done, such as live a good life or a religious life, or you will tell Him that you are persuaded that there is nothing you have done that qualifies you for heaven, but you are trusting Jesus, who did everything necessary that qualifies you for heaven when He died to pay for your sins and rose from the dead.

The Bible says, "not by works of righteousness which we have done, but according to His mercy He saved us" (Titus 3:5). "For by grace you have been saved through faith, and that not of yourselves; it is the gift of God, not of works, lest anyone should boast" (Ephesians 2:8-9).

Well, are you persuaded? If you haven't done so already, from this moment, trust Jesus Christ, plus nothing else, to get to heaven.

APPENDIX

EARLY REFERENCES TO THE NEW TESTAMENT

Shortly after the completion of the New Testament (AD 95), ancient authors quoted or alluded to it, which indicates New Testament books existed and, in many cases, were considered authoritative and even inspired. Clement (AD 95) reminds the Corinthians that "the blessed apostle Paul" wrote to them "under the inspiration of the spirit" (1 Clement, Chapter 47). So, after the New Testament was written, it was considered inspired (1 Tim. 5:18; 2 Pet. 15-16, Clement).

See the overview chart on the next page.

Conclusion

NT Book	NT Reference	Ancient Author	Reference
Matthew	6:25	Diognetu(AD 100)	Chapter 9
	7:1	Polycarp (AD 110)	Chapter 2
Mark	9:42; 14:21	Clement (AD 95)	Chapter 46
Luke	10:7	Paul (AD 63)	1 Timothy 5:18
John	17:11, 14, 16	Diognetus(AD 100)	Chapter 6
Acts	20:35	Clement (AD 95)	Chapter 2
Romans	9:5/1:32	Clement (AD 95)	Chapter 31/35
	14:10-12	Polycarp (AD 110)	Chapter 6
1 Corinthians	Paul wrote under inspiration	Clement (AD 95)	Chapter 47
2 Corinthians	10:3; 6:10	Diognetus (AD 100)	Chapter 5
Galatians	2:9	Clement (AD 95)	Chapter 5
	4:10	Diognetus (AD100)	Chapter 4
Ephesians	4:4-6	Clement (AD 95)	Chapter 46
Philippians	3:20 Study Paul's letter to you	Diognetus(AD 100)	Chapter 5
		Polycarp (AD 110)	Chapter 3
Colossians	1:18	Clement (AD 95)	Chapter 24
1 Thessalonians	5:17/5:22	Polycarp (AD 110)	Chapter 4/11
2 Thessalonians	3:15	Polycarp (AD 110)	Chapter 11
1 Timothy	3:16	Diognetus(AD 100)	Chapter 11
	6;7, 10	Polycarp (AD 110)	Chapter 4
2 Timothy	1:3	Clement (AD 95)	Chapter 45
	2:12	Polycarp (AD 110)	Chapter 5
Titus	3:1/2:10	Clement (AD 95)	Chapter 2/26
Philemon	20	Ignatius (AD 116)	Ephesians II
Hebrews	1:2, 3, 4, 6, 13/3:5/11:37	Clement (AD 95)	Chapter 36/43/17
James	3:13	Clement (AD 95)	Chapter 38
1 Peter	1:19/4:8	Clement (AD 95)	Chapter 7/49
2 Peter	3:15	Polycarp (AD 110)	Chapter 3
1 John	4:2-3	Polycarp (AD 110)	Chapter 7
2 John	May be included with 1 Jn.	Irenaeus	
3 John	May be included with 1 Jn.	Irenaeus	
Jude	3/20	Polycarp (AD 110)	Chapter 3
Revelation	22:12	Clement (AD 95)	Chapter 34

BIBLIOGRAPHY

Abbott-Smith, G. *A Manual Greek Lexicon of the New Testament.* Edinburgh: T & T. Clark, 1960.

Aland, Kurt; Aland, Barbara. *The Text of the New Testament. An Introduction to the Critical Editions and to the Theory and Practice of Modern Textual Criticism.* Grand Rapids: William B Erdman Publishing Company, 1995.

Alford, Henry. *The Greek New Testament.* Revised by Everett F. Harrison. Chicago: Moody Press, 1958.

Archer, Gleason. *A Survey of the Old Testament.* Grand Rapids: Wm. B. Eerdmans, 1962.

Arndt, William and Gingrich, F. Wilbur, translated by Walter Bauer. *A Greek-English Lexicon of the New Testament and Other Early Christian Literature.* Chicago: The University of Chicago Press. 1979.

Baker, Charles F. *A Dispensational Theology.* Grand Rapids: Grace Bible College Publications, 1971.

Baldwin, Joyce G. Daniel. *Tyndale Old Testament Series.* Downer Grove, IL: Intervarsity Press, 1978.

Beckwith, R. T. *Old Testament Canon of the New Testament Church and its Background in Early Judaism.* Grand Rapids: Eerdmans, 1985.

Black, David Alan. *Rethinking New Testament Textual Criticism.* Grand Rapids' Baker Book House, 2002.

Borland, James A. "Re-examining the Textual-Critical Principles and Practices Used to Negate Inerrancy," *The Journal of the Evangelical Theological Society*, vol. 25, December 1982.

Boutflower, Charles. *In and Around the Book of Daniel*. Grand Rapids: Zondervan Publishing House, 1963.

Bruce, F. F. *The Canon of Scripture*. Downer Grove, IL: Intervarsity Press, 1988.

_____ *The New Testament Documents Are They Reliable?* Downer Grove, IL: Intervarsity Press, 1984.

Burgon, John. *The Last Twelve Verses of Mark*. Grand Rapids: Associated Publishers and Authors, n. d.

_____ *The Revision Revised*. Paradise, Pa.: Conservative Classics, reprint, n. d.

_____ *Unholy Hands on the Bible,* vol. 1. The Complete Works of John W. Burgon. Lafayette, IN: Sovereign Grace Trust Fund, 1990.

Bush, George. *Notes on Joshua*. New York: Newman & Ivison. 1852. Reprinted by James and Klock Publishing of Minneapolis in 1976.

Cairns, Earle E. *Christianity Through the Century*. Grand Rapids: Zondervan, 1981.

Campbell, Donald K. *No Time for Neutrality*. Wheaton: Victor Books, 1981.

Campenhausen, Hans von. *The Formation of the Christian Bible*. Translated by J. A. Baker. Mifflintown, PA: Sigler Press, 1977.

Carson, D. A. *The King James Version Debate*. Grand Rapids: Baker Book House, 1979.

Chafer, Lewis Sperry, *Systematic Theology*. Dallas: Dallas Seminary Press, 1947.

Delitzsch, Franz. *Biblical Commentary on Isaiah*. Translated by Francis Bolton. Biblical Commentary on the Old Testament. N.p.; reprint ed., Grand Rapids: Wm. B. Eerdmans Publishing Co., n.d. e-sword.net edition.

Ehrman, Bart D. "After the New Testament: The Writings of the Apostolic Fathers," *Audio Lectures and Course Guidebook.* Chantilly, Virginia: The Teaching Company, 2005.

Ewert, David. *From Ancient Tablets to Modern Translations: A General Introduction to the Bible.* Grand Rapids: Zondervan, 1983.

Ellis, E. E. *The Old Testament in Early Christianity.* Grand Rapids: Baker Book House, 2002.

Farnell, David F. "The Synoptic Gospels in the Ancient Church: A Testimony to the Priority of Matthew's Gospel." *The Master's Seminary Journal,* 10:1 (1999).

Farstad, Arthur L. *The New King James Version: In the Great Tradition.* Nashville: Thomas Nelson Publishers, 1989.

Fuller, David Otis. *Which Bible?* Grand Rapids: Grand Rapids International Publications, 1971.

Geisler, Norman L. *Christian Apologetics.* Peabody, MA: Prince Press, 2002.

Gill, John. *John Gill's Exposition of the Bible.* e-sword.net.

Green, Sr., Jay. *Unholy Hands on the Bible. The Complete Works of John W. Burgon.* Volume 1. Lafayette, IN: Sovereign Grace Trust Fund, 1990. Green wrote the Preface.

Harrison, Everett F. *Introduction to the New Testament.* Grand Rapids: William B. Eerdmans Publishing Company, 1968.

Harrison, Roland Kenneth. *Introduction to the Old Testament.* Grand Rapids: Wm. B. Eerdmans, 1969.

Hendricksen, William. *New Testament Commentary: Exposition of the Pastoral Epistles.* Reprint ed. Grand Rapids: Baker Book House, 1968.

Hiebert, D. Edmond. *An Introduction to the Non-Pauline Epistle.* Chicago: Moody Press, 1969.

_____ *First Timothy*. Moody Colportage Library series. Chicago: Moody Press, 1957.

Hill, C. E. "The Debate over the Muratorian Fragment and the Development of the Canon," *Westminster Theological Journal*, 57:2, Fall 199, pp. 437-452.

Hills, Edward F. *King James Version Defended*. Des Moines, Iowa: The Christian Research Press, 1956.

Hodges, Zane C. "Introduction to the Textus Receptus." Unpublished Notes, n.d.

_____ "The Angel at Bethesda—John 5:4." *Bibliotheca Sacra* 136:541 (January-March 1979), 25-39.

_____ "The Greek Text of the King James Version." *Bibliotheca Sacra*, 125:500 (Oct -Dec 1968)' 334-345.

_____; Farstad, Arthur L. *The Greek New Testament According to the Majority Text*. Nashville: Thomas Nelson Publishers, 1982.

_____; Radmacher, Earl. *The NIV Reconsidered*. Dallas Redención Viva, 1990.

Kistemaker, Simon J. "The Canon of the New Testament." *Journal of the Evangelical Theological Society*, 20/1, Winter, 1977.

Keil C. F., and Delitzsch F. *Biblical Commentary on the Books of Samuel*. Grand Rapids: Wm. B. Eerdmans, 1962.

Kelly, J. N. D. *Early Christian Doctrines*. Peabody, MA, Prince Press, 2003.

Kent, Homer A., Jr. *The Pastoral Epistles. Chicago*: Moody Press, 1966.

Kruger, Michael J. *The Early Text of the New Testament*. Oxford: Oxford University Press, 2014.

Laetsch, Theo. *Jeremiah*. Saint Louis: Concordia Publishing House, 1965.

Leiman, Sid Z. *The Canonization of Hebrew Scripture: The Talmudic and Midrashic Evidence*. Hamden, Conn.: Archon Books, 1976.

Lightfoot, J. B. *Notes on the Epistles of St. Paul*. Reprint ed. Winona Lake, Ind.: Alpha Publications, n.d.

Mayor, Joseph B., *The Epistle of St. James*. London: Macmillan and Co., 1897.

McDonald, Lee Martin, *The Biblical Canon*. Peabody, MA: Hendrickson, 2008.

McDowell, Josh. *New Evidence That Demands a Verdict*. Nashville: Thomas Nelson Publishers, 1999.

Metzger, Bruce M. *The Text of the New Testament: Its Transmission, Corruption, and Restoration*, 3rd ed. 1992.

Miller, H. S., *General Biblical Introduction*. Houghton, NY: The Word Bearer Press, 1947.

Nicole, Roger. "The Canon of the New Testament," *Journal of the Evangelical Theological Society*, vol. 40, June 1997, pp. 199-206.

Pickering, Wilbur N. *The Greek New Testament According to Family 35*. Second Edition. Creative Commons Attribution-ShareAlike, 2015.

_____ and Freitas, Marcelo. *Family 35*. Creative Commons Attribution-ShareAlike, 2021.

Ridderbos, Herman. *The Authority of the New Testament Scriptures*. Philadelphia: Presbyterian & Reformed Publishing Co., 1963.

Robinson, Maurice A. and Pierpont, William G. *The New Testament in the original Greek*. Nurnberg, Germany: VTR publishers, 2018.

Ruchman, Peter. *The Christian's Handbook of Manuscript Evidence*. Pensacola: Bible Press, 1990.

Ryrie, Charles C. *Basic Theology*. Wheaton, Illinois: Victor Books, 1986.

Sawyer, M. James. "Evangelicals and the Canon of the New Testament," *Grace Theological Journal*, vol. 11, #1, Spring 1990, pp. 29-52.

Sheeley, Steven M. "From 'Scripture' to 'Canon': the Development of the New Testament Canon," *Review and Expositor*, vol. 95:4, Fall 1998.

Sorensen, David H. *Neither Oldest Nor Best*: Duluth, MN: North Star Ministries, 2019.

Sturz, A. Harry. *The Byzantine Text type in New Testament Textual Criticism*. Nashville: Thomas Nelson Publishers, 1984.

Tenney, Merrill C. *The New Testament: An Historical and Analytic Survey*. Grand Rapids: Wm. B. Eerdmans, 1960.

The New Testament, *The Greek Text Underlying the English Authorized Version of 1611*. London: The Trinitarian Bible Society, 1976.

Thiessen, Henry C. *Introduction to the New Testament*. Grand Rapids: Wm. B. Eerdmans, 1962.

Thompson, J. A. *The Book of Jeremiah, The New International Commentary on the Old Testament,* Grand Rapids: Wm. B. Eerdmans, 1987.

Unger, Merrill F. *Introductory Guide to the Old Testament*. Grand Rapids: Zondervan Publishing House, 1956.

Wallace, Daniel. "Did the Original New Testament Manuscripts still exist in the Second Century?". *Bibliotheca Sacra* (April-June) 1991.

_____. *Speech on New Testament Manuscripts*, 2013. The speech is posted at http://marturiamine.blogspot.com/2013/09/confession-of-ex-tr-evangelist.html.

Wallace, J. Warner. *Cold Case-Christianity*. Colorado Springs: David C. Cook, 2013.

Warfield, B. B. *The Inspiration and Authority of the Bible,* Grand Rapids: Baker Book House, 1981.

Wayne, Luke. "Differences Between the Majority Text and the Textus Receptus." https://carm.org/king-james-onlyism/differences-between-the-majority-text-and-the-textus-receptus/

Westcott, B. F. *A General Survey of the History of the Canon of the New Testament*. London: MacMillan, 1855; 6th edition 1889; reprinted, Grand Rapids, 1980.

Westcott, Brooke Foss and Hort, Fenton John Anthony. *New Testament in the Original Greek, Introduction and Appendix.* New York: Harper and Brothers, Franklin Square, 1882, reprint edition by Forgotten Books, 2012.

White, James R. *The King James Only Controversy*. Minneapolis: Bethany House Publishers, 1995.

Wood, Leon. *A Commentary on Daniel*. Grand Rapids: Regency Reference Library, 1973.

Woudstra M. H. *The Book of Joshua*, The New International Commentary on the Old Testament, Grand Rapids: Wm. B. Eerdmans, 1985.

Woudstra, Sierd. "A Teacher Looks at the NIV." *The Banner* 124 (April 10, 1989) 8-9.

Yarborough, Robert W. "The Date of Papias: A Reassessment," Journal of the *Evangelical Theological Society*, vol. 26, pp. 181-82.

Young, E. J. "The Canon of the Old Testament," *Revelation and the Bible*, p. 168.

About The Author

G. Michael Cocoris is a gifted communicator. He can make even complicated subjects simple, clear, and practical. His breadth of experience has allowed him to relate to a wide range of audiences.

Michael received a Bachelor of Arts degree from Tennessee Temple University, a Master of Theology degree from Dallas Seminary, and a Doctorate of Divinity from Biola University. He traveled the United States for over a dozen years as a speaker. He has also been a seminary professor, visiting lecturer, and world traveler, including hosting tours to Israel and China.

Michael has pastored three churches, including a rural church when he was in seminary, an urban church, the historic Church of the Open Door, first in downtown Los Angeles and later in Glendora, California, and a suburban church, the Lindley Church in Tarzana California, a suburb of Los Angeles. While at the Church of Open Door, he had a daily radio broadcast.

Michael has written numerous magazine articles, mainly for *Biblical Research Monthly*. He has authored a number of books, including *Seventy Years on Hope Street, A History of the Church of the Open Door*; *How To Live A Biblical Spiritual Life, Clarifying the Confusion; Repentance, The Most Misunderstood Word in the Bible; Evangelism: A Biblical Approach; The Salvation Controversy; Lordship Salvation: Is It Biblical?; The Books of the Bible, the Subject, Structure, Situation, and Significant Verses of Each Book; Psalms, A Song for Every Situation, Each Summarized on One Page; and Counseling Theories, A Biblical Evaluation.* In addition, he was a contributor to The *NKJV Study Bible* and *Nelson's New Illustrated Bible Commentary*.

Michael is the pastor of the Lindley Church in Tarzana, California. He and his wife, Patricia, live in Santa Monica, California.

www.ingramcontent.com/pod-product-compliance
Lightning Source LLC
Chambersburg PA
CBHW070106080526
44586CB00013B/1201